Advertising for A Small Business Made Simple

Bernard Ryan, Jr.

Edited and prepared for publication by New England Publishing Associates, Inc.

A Made Simple Book
DOUBLEDAY New York London Toronto Sydney Auckland

ACKNOWLEDGMENTS

Particular thanks go to O. Burtch Drake, president and CEO of the American Association of Advertising Agencies (A.A.A.A.), and to Joyce Harrington, A.A.A.A. senior vice president/public affairs. And for their help in retrieving valuable resource information, many thanks to Marsha Appel, A.A.A.A. vice president and manager of its Member Information Service (MIS), and to Marge Morris, assistant manager of MIS.

— BR, Jr.

A MADE SIMPLE BOOK

PUBLISHED BY DOUBLEDAY
a division of Bantam Doubleday Dell Publishing Group, Inc.
1540 Broadway, New York, New York 10036

MADE SIMPLE and DOUBLEDAY are trademarks of Doubleday,
a division of Bantam Doubleday Dell Publishing Group, Inc.

NEW ENGLAND
PUBLISHING
ASSOCIATES

Edited and prepared for publication by
New England Publishing Associates, Inc.

Principals: Elizabeth Frost Knappman & Edward W. Knappman

Staff:
Rebecca Barardy
Larry Hand
Victoria Harlow
Romanie Rout
David Voytek

Copy Editor:
Joanne Wlodarczyk

Page Composition:
Teri Prestash

Proofreader:
Margaret Heinrich Hand

Library of Congress Cataloging-in-Publication Data
Ryan, Bernard Jr. 1923—
Advertising for a small business made simple/Bernard Ryan Jr.; edited and prepared for publication by New England Publishing Associates, Inc.
p. cm.
"A Made Simple Book."
Includes bibliographical references and index.
1. Advertising 2. Small Business I. Title.
HF5823.R878 1996
659.1—dc20 95-11876
ISBN 0-385-47556-X

PRINTED IN THE UNITED STATES OF AMERICA
1996
FIRST EDITION

10 9 8 7 6 5 4 3 2 1

CONTENTS

PART ONE

WHAT IS ADVERTISING AND HOW DOES IT WORK?

"I will find me a business that does not advertise," said the wise spider, "and I will weave my web across its doorway, for there I will be undisturbed."

— Attributed to Mark Twain

CHAPTER ONE

Advertising Is Communication

KEY TERMS

attributes	*effectiveness*	*objectives*
awareness	*image*	*sensory register*
benefit	*long-term storage*	*short-term memory*
competition	*marketing mix*	*strategy*
consumer		

Are you a small-business advertiser? That depends, of course, on whether or not your company is a small business. According to the Small Business Administration, your company is a small business if it employs fewer than 500 people. Dun & Bradstreet, on the other hand, defines a small business as any business that has 50 or fewer employees.

With the help of Response Analysis Corp., Dun & Bradstreet has extensively studied small businesses. It sees a qualitative difference between small companies employing more than 50 employees and those employing 50 or fewer: The owners and CEOs of the smaller companies make most of the major decisions. Once a company has more than 50 employees, the owner or CEO is forced to give up hands-on involvement. He or she has to hire department heads or managers to handle sales and marketing, personnel and employee benefits, finance and credit, and cash flow.

Dun & Bradstreet's study also found that the majority of owners and CEOs of *very* small businesses—those with fewer than

25 employees—like to do most things themselves. They don't turn to outsiders for help in such areas as sales and marketing. The only exception? They will ask industry associations and trade groups for advice.

Other findings: Those who own and run small businesses like to share information with others in the same line of work. They depend on word of mouth and referrals to bring in new business. Most of them have made no plans for the future. And few have ever worked up a marketing plan.

Does some or all of this describe you? Are you the owner or CEO of a small company, and do you make the decisions and handle the marketing and advertising yourself? Or are you a department head or manager in a business employing fewer than 500 people, and are you responsible for your company's marketing and advertising? If so, this book was written for you, because whatever the size of your small business, a well-thought-out marketing and advertising plan is vital to its success.

Overview: What's It All About?

Advertising is a mode of communication from someone who is providing a product or service to someone who is, or is likely to be, a customer. The communication, in almost all cases, is a sales message. If you are offering something for sale, you can usually reach more prospective buyers through advertising than you can any other way—and you can do it more efficiently and more effectively.

Effectiveness means sales. And profits. How you make sales and gain profits through advertising is directly related to how well you discipline yourself in developing your advertising strategy. And whether your advertising strategy will be on target—or not on target—depends on how thoroughly you analyze your product or service, your **competition,** and your **consumer** and how well you figure out exactly *what* you need to say in your advertising...all before you start to work on *how* to say it.

When you buy advertising, what are you paying for? You're buying the chance to have potential customers see and hear what you have to say about the products or services you are selling. What you say must be helpful and useful and informative to the potential customer, or you are wasting your money. And what you say must be more helpful and more useful and more informative than the message your competitor is sending to that same potential customer.

In other words, your advertising must set your store or business apart from all the others, characterizing it in some way that makes it unique, and it must do this in a way that grabs the attention of the reader, listener, or viewer. If the advertising that depicts your business as unique is more helpful, more useful, and more informative than that of your competitor, and if it gets attention, it should result in sales. And profits.

Where do you start? Think about a deliberate management goal: to create advertising that sells. Think about what makes your store or business different. Look at your current advertising. Does it address what makes your store or business different? Think about who creates your advertising. Do your creative people have your confidence and support? Can they take some risks, try new ideas, probe ways to communicate the unique qualities of your store or product or service?

The purpose of this book is to help you understand all these factors and to guide you toward "yes" answers to all these questions.

Advertising: One Element of Marketing

Before you can develop a successful advertising plan or **strategy,** you must have a sound marketing plan. Chapter 3 will describe the marketing plan in detail, but think now about how you market your product or service. Do you see your product as the consumer sees it? What does it do for the buyer? What problem does it solve? What is the primary benefit your customer gets from it? Other benefits? Can the product be changed to reduce its cost or to improve its attractiveness or to make it more competitive?

Next, look at the price. Is it competitive? Is the consumer willing to pay your price? Can you increase the price, to gain a wider profit margin? Or can you cut it to increase sales volume?

Now consider distribution. Do you make sure your product is where the consumer can get it when he or she wants it? If you are selling a service, can you provide it on your customer's timetable? Can you cut costs by changing your method of distribution or increase sales volume by making your product or service more easily available? If you are a retailer, does your store stock what a typical customer expects to find in a store like yours?

Finally, think about promotion. Are you telling your customers about the benefits of your product or service in a way that is persuasive and competitive? And is the message going to the right potential customers?

All these elements—your product, price, distribution, and promotion—work together in what is known as the **marketing mix.** Before you can successfully work out an advertising plan, you must look carefully at all aspects of your marketing mix and figure out what marketing problems you have. Then you must fix them—unless you see a way for advertising to fix them.

When your marketing problems are under control, and only then, it is time to develop an advertising plan or strategy.

Why Are You Advertising?

Are you advertising to make sales? Certainly. But that's a generality. Think about your specific **objectives** and write them down. If you are a retailer, your primary objective may be to build traffic—to get as many customers as possible into your store. That's the first objective of most retailers. If you make an established product or offer an established service, your primary objective may be to find new customers. Or to introduce a new product to existing customers. Or to suggest a new way for existing customers to use a product they already know and love. Or to take customers away from a competitor. The variations on such basic objectives are almost endless.

There are other objectives, too. They range from motivating your employees to perform better to justifying a price that is higher than your competitor's to influencing the opinion of the man or woman in the street about your company, store, or shopping center or even your entire industry.

The purpose of getting down to specific objectives for advertising is to force yourself to think about who your customer is—and why. Who is going to buy? When? Where? And how? To work out a successful advertising plan or strategy, you must know what specific results you expect. Then, when you invest money in advertising, you will be investing wisely, with a specific purpose in mind.

What Are You Selling?

If you are a small-business advertiser, chances are more than likely that you are selling something in either of two broad categories. One is retailing—the sale of products or services directly to the consumer. The other is business-to-business—the sale of products or services that other businesses need in order to produce their products or services for sale to their consumers.

"All politics is local," said Tip O'Neill, the late Speaker of the U.S. House of Representatives. He could have said the same thing about all retail advertising. Retailers constitute the most significant group in advertising. Local advertisers are companies, businesses, or establishments that serve consumers rather than other businesses and that operate in a relatively small geographic area, such as a single city or county. What do they sell? By far the largest group of retailers is food stores. Next, ranked by sales, come new car dealers, restaurants and bars, and gas stations. Then discount stores, followed by department, drug, building supply, women's wear, auto supply, furniture, and electronics stores. Those are the top 12 categories in retail sales; the total sales of the nation's 2.68 million retail stores amount to nearly $3 trillion annually.

As you know if you are one of them, retail businesses are changing—fast. Thanks to computer hardware and software and vast databases of information on consumers, retailers can now closely track their present customers and target new ones. They are finding out that, more and more, consumers are "time poor." They don't want to bother even coming to the store, let alone spending much time there. Their time is spent with television or on the job. They are choosing brands and stores they feel they can trust. Retailers are learning that, in building relationships with customers, quality of service and delivery of value are stronger factors than price. Retailers look hard for ways to tell *their* customers that there is something unique about their store that won't be found at the competitor down the street or across the mall.

No less an authority than the well-known economist Peter F. Drucker has offered timely advice on the future of retailing:

> Shopping is becoming a chore and it is a job of the successful retailer not to make it enjoyable, but to make it, I wouldn't say the least painful but, the least burdensome, the least complicated and bluntly the least important, where the traditional approach was to make shopping important...
>
> The new retailers' approach is that shopping is something that has to be

done and it's our job to enable them to do it so that it is least important to them, least demanding, least time consuming. I am not saying that this has happened. I am not even saying that this is going to happen. I'm only saying that this might well happen, and that it's a trend that I would, if I were a retailer, pay the most attention to.

So here are some observations of an old friend, who is an outsider, who is not a retailer, but who has been watching the retail economy, the distribution economy for a long time. Let me say that one thing is very certain: More is happening in retailing than is happening in manufacturing or in finance. It is retailing distribution which in the next few years is going to be the area of the greatest innovations and greatest changes.[1]

But what if you're in business-to-business selling? In this second broad category of small-business advertising, you are selling not to the consumer who takes your product home—or uses your service at home—but to a customer who is buying your product or service for business use. This category includes four specific types of advertising:

- *Industrial advertising.* Here you are selling your product to businesses that will incorporate it into their products. Or you are selling something that will help them manufacture their products or operate their businesses more easily.
- *Trade advertising.* This advertising is directed to resellers, wholesalers, and retailers. You run trade advertising to persuade these businesses to stock your product for resale to consumers.
- *Professional advertising.* Your target here is doctors, lawyers, accountants, management consultants, architects—anyone who may be in a position to advise others to buy or use your product or service.
- *Agricultural advertising.* If you are in this market, you are making products and offering services that are needed by farmers large or small.

If you are selling in any of these areas, your advertising needs to generate **awareness** of your name, project a memorable **image** of your company, and position your firm vis-à-vis your competition. It should also provide information about your product or service to prospective customers, announce technological innovations and new products, tell your prospects about promotions and special programs, pull in inquiries, and open the door so your salespeople can make sales calls.

Why Are They Buying?

Whether you are selling business-to-business or directly to the consumer, there is only one reason why your customer is buying: There is something in it for him or her. What is that something? It is a **benefit.**

A benefit is not how well you made your product, or what ingenious parts or expensive ingredients you put into it, or the fact that some authority figure or celebrity has already bought it and loves it and recommends it. Those—and countless other reasons for buying that are offered by advertisers—are simply **attributes.** A benefit, on the other hand, is a lifetime guarantee (because you made the product so well) or a taste that your customer will want to enjoy

1. Drucker, Peter F. "Retailing in a Post-Capitalist Society." *Stores,* August 1993, 4. Reproduced by permission of the author.

again and again (because of the expensive ingredients you put into your product). The only genuine function of an authority figure or celebrity in advertising is to draw attention to the message. If he or she does not then offer a benefit to the prospective buyer, the message is useless.

In brief, your customers are buying because, from your advertising, they perceive benefits for themselves. Therefore, your advertising must take the customer's point of view and promise benefits. In most cases, the benefits provide solutions to problems. A classic advertising saying sums up this idea: Consumers don't buy quarter-inch drills, they buy quarter-inch holes.

But How Does Advertising Work?

Experts who have studied the psychology of communication say that how advertising works is highly dependent upon how the message is accepted in our heads, stored there, and later retrieved when we make decisions.

The information coming in to us, whether it is advertising or anything else, is processed through three systems that store it. The first is called the **sensory register.** It receives the information and in a flash sorts it into shapes and sounds and forms, getting the information instantly ready for processing. Next, the information goes into **short-term memory**—a very active area where the information stays only long enough for some reasoning and rapid judgment to take place. Third, the information moves into **long-term storage.** Here is stored every piece of information we have ever processed. Most of it, obviously, is not in current use.

That middle stage—short-term memory—is the vital one, for it is the gate to the third stage. Any information that comes in from advertising must have enough strength and pertinence to the individual to pass through the judgment gate and into the long-term memory. Otherwise it is tossed out. Forgotten.

But then, any advertising information that reaches the long-term memory must compete for acceptance with information that has already been through the process and been deposited in long-term storage. If and when the new information is accepted, it then waits to be retrieved.

When we think about buying any product or service, we are prompted by either a want or a need. A need is something we cannot get along without—food and clothing, shelter and security, transportation. A want is something we could get along without if we had to—any upscale, fancier, or more expensive version of an item in the basic need categories or just about anything else that we do not need in order to survive. Dinner is a need. Dining out is a want. For most Americans, an automobile is a need. A BMW is a want. Kmart supplies most needs (and plenty of wants), while Neiman-Marcus supplies mostly wants and very few needs.

The psychologists tell us that wants and needs are either active or latent. When a need or a want is active, we are aware of it and are trying to do something about it. When either of these is latent, it is lying around in the back of the mind, waiting to be stirred up.

An example? When your shoes wear out, you know it. You go shopping for "actively needed" shoes. When you pass a shoe store in the mall just after payday and see an attractive pair of shoes in the window, you retrieve a latent want. You go in and buy the shoes that satisfy this latent want but that are not an absolute need.

People make either of two kinds of decisions: rational or emotional. You buy the *needed* shoes based on utility—how well they are made, how long they are expected to last—and on price. But the emotional side affects the decision: If you feel that "these shoes just don't do a thing for me," you ask the salesperson to show you something else. On the other hand, you buy the *wanted* shoes based on what they will do for your self-esteem—how well they will go with the outfit you're wearing Saturday night—and maybe on price. But you let the rational side in on the decision: If you feel that "these shoes are too uncomfortable to dance in," you ask to see another pair.

When you think about your advertising, think about where your product or service fits into your prospective customer's complex of active and latent needs and wants. Think about what any person who is deciding to buy something goes through. Is the buyer looking to meet an active need or to satisfy a latent want? Is his or her decision going to be a rational one or an emotional one? And don't forget—your customer or prospect is not *consciously* going through all this. It is pretty much a subconscious process. But you should be aware of it, in terms of whatever you are selling and your desire to advertise it in a way that produces sales.

That's not all the buyer goes through, subconsciously or consciously. Your buyer perceives that choosing your product or service will bring a benefit. Choosing means considering alternatives...like going to your competitors. Making the choice means deciding that your product or service will do the job better than your competitors' will. It also means that the choice will be acceptable—to family and friends, if you are selling to the consumer, or to business associates, if you are selling business-to-business. Finally, choosing your product means that your customer believes it will conform to his or her self-image. These three aspects of choice—effectiveness, acceptance by others, and approval by oneself—are areas of risk. The buyer weighs, usually subconsciously, the risk involved in each area: What if it doesn't work right? What if my family doesn't want it or like it? How is it going to make me feel?

All this psychological background points to one basic conclusion: Advertising is for experts. It is not for amateurs. You can become an expert, or you can call on experts to help you. The important thing is that you spend your advertising dollars to present your advertising message clearly and effectively so that you build a continuing relationship with your audience or market. Don't forget as you create individual advertisements that you are also creating an overall, long-term impression about your store or product or service. And that is equally important.

Now, here you are, ready and eager to put your advertising before your prospects. What must your ad say, when and where must it appear to have the greatest influence? And what can the advertising business do to help you?

Summary

Advertising is a mode of communication. When it is effective, it produces sales by finding a way to catch potential customers' attention and show them your business is unique. But before you begin creating advertising, you must develop a sound marketing plan. A marketing plan analyzes your particular marketing mix and uncovers marketing problems. Next, set down objectives you want your advertising to address, along with the results you expect to achieve. Think about what you are selling, either as a retailer or as a business-to-business marketer. Think about what your customer is buying. What is the benefit to be gained from buying your product or service? And think about how the human mind processes and stores information and how, in making decisions, it subconsciously sorts out wants and needs and weighs rational and emotional factors.

CHAPTER TWO

The Advertising Business

KEY TERMS

advertiser
agency
à la carte services
cable television
compensation arrangements
direct response
electronic media
in-house
media
media commissions
out-of-home
print
production
public relations
rate card
sales promotion
space
tasks
time
transit advertising

Before getting into the nitty-gritty of who does what (and where, when, how, and why they do it), take a look at the advertising business in an overall sense. It will be valuable to you to understand the various elements that work together to form the advertising industry, so you can see where you and your business fit in and how you can use the industry most effectively.

The advertising industry consists of three broad segments: advertisers, advertising agencies, and the media. In addition, the business extends its reach to include the direct response media, sales promotion activities, and public relations endeavors. The role of each of these segments is described in subsequent chapters of this book, but let's look at them briefly now so you can get an idea of who's who and what's what in the business.

What Is an Advertiser?

If you run a business that needs to attract prospective customers, if you wish you could presell your prospects on the merits of your company's products or services before your salespeople make calls, if you want to generate inquiries about what you are selling, if you are introducing new or improved products or services to your market, if you are expanding your business by entering a new market, if your business suffers from seasonal fluctuations in sales, if your competition seems to grab sales you thought were yours, if your business needs to build goodwill—if any of these "ifs" describes your situation, you are or should be an advertiser.

An **advertiser** is any individual or firm that buys time or space in any medium of communication in order to get a message to those who read, watch, or listen to that medium. It is understood that when we use the word *advertising,* we mean that a fee is paid for the privilege of appearing in the medium. If no money changes hands, it's not advertising.

Nearly half of all advertisers are local businesses and retailers, ranging from department stores to supermarkets, from car dealers to banks. After many decades of having placed advertising in the traditional media (mostly newspapers and radio), these businesses have recently begun spending more and more of their advertising budgets in such new media as cable television and direct response techniques. A recent study of a typical cross-section of such advertisers revealed that 81 percent were independently owned businesses; the others were parts of chains or franchises. For 53 percent of these small businesses, the monthly advertising budget was $2,000 or less, while 47 percent spent more than $2,000.

What Is an Advertising Agency?

An advertising **agency** is a service business that takes responsibility for creating advertising messages and placing them with the media. This responsibility may be for one or for many tasks, including not only creative work and planning and buying the media but research; production; direct response; sales promotion; package design; public relations; dealer aids; planning sales meetings, exhibitions, and special events; product testing; and advising on marketing strategy. (See Chapter 6.)

You will have a tough time finding any other relationship between two separate and independent businesses that is as intimate and as dependent on partnership as that between an advertiser and its agency. If you want the relationship to be successful, you must entrust your agency with the proprietary information it needs to fulfill its responsibilities to you. You must think of your agency not as a vendor but as a partner.

As Chapter 6 discusses in greater detail, working in partnership with an advertising agency can bring you any number of benefits. You gain the agency's experience, usually far greater than your own, in the planning of marketing and of strategic advertising. You get the advantage of an outsider's objective viewpoint on your business problems and opportunities. Skills in the creation of exciting, attention-getting advertising and in its placement in the most appropriate media come with the agency. In addition, you get expertise in research and production techniques and are relieved of the more mundane housekeeping chores—

budget and cost control and trafficking of advertising materials to the media. In other words, you don't have to worry about *coordinating* your entire advertising program when you develop a working partnership with an advertising agency.

Must You Use an Agency?

Not every advertiser uses an agency. You may find it advantageous to handle your advertising program in either of two other ways. The first is by buying **à la carte services.** You can find independent resources that provide any of the individual elements of your advertising program. Creative boutiques specialize in conceptualizing your advertising campaign, writing the copy (the words that are read or heard by your audience), and designing the art (the graphic "look" of your ads in the print or out-of-home media or on television). Media-buying groups plan and execute the placement of your advertising. Other independent firms provide strategic marketing planning, product positioning, **production** (photography, videotaping, filming, etc.), talent negotiation, sales promotion, direct response, research, public relations—you name it. You can pick and choose those services you want and need from many sources. Many advertisers find that by buying services à la carte, they can get a quicker response, greater objectivity, more instantaneous communication, and superior talent. Some also claim that their ultimate cost is lower via the à la carte route than any other way.

There is one catch, however. When you buy services à la carte, the coordination is up to you. You have to do all the planning and management that keep the program on schedule. To some advertisers, this responsibility comes with the territory. They don't believe in delegating such responsibilities.

The second alternative to working in partnership with an agency is to handle your advertising program entirely **in-house.** This means adding staff, hiring people on salary to handle all the tasks involved in putting your advertising before your audience. Why do advertisers move their programs in-house? Usually they think it will save them money and improve efficiency in the purchasing of advertising materials and services. Experts who have studied this have found that efficiency may indeed improve in some situations. Department stores, for example, have traditionally maintained in-house advertising staffs, which become proficient in producing volumes of advertising (traditionally in newspapers) day after day. But you need just that—a steady volume of work to keep your staff busy full-time—to justify setting up an in-house advertising department.

Cost reduction is a questionable claim. If you want to hire for your in-house operation people whose talents and skills are comparable to those in agencies or at à la carte services, you will have to pay them well. In addition, your own indirect or overhead costs are likely to be just as high as those of your agency. And, at the same time, you will still have a significant drawback: You will miss out on the objectivity that the outsider brings. You will run the risk that your in-house people will be subject to undue influence from the company management, and they will lose their consumer-oriented point of view. Not only that, but your in-house staffers will not be gaining the broad experience that comes from working with other products and services, experience that agency or à la carte service people constantly build on.

So Whom Do You Pay to Get Your Message Across?

You pay the media. You pay the agency. You pay the à la carte services.

The **media** are all the methods of communication by which your message is carried to the public for a fee. They include

- **Electronic media.** Broadcast television and radio head this group. But **cable television** is growing rapidly.
- **Print.** Daily, weekly, and Sunday newspapers have long been the foundation media for retail advertising. Newspapers have so strongly dominated the retail advertising world for so many decades that it is only now beginning to dawn on newspaper publishers and on advertisers that today there are other equally effective—if not, in fact, *more* effective—media.

  Magazines are the other main category of print media. They include publications aimed at consumers, such as general-interest, news, special-interest (hobbies, sports, cars), and men's and women's magazines. Then there are business and trade publications. Some are horizontal publications, for readers who hold the same or similar positions in various industries (for example, purchasing agents). Others are vertical publications, those aimed at people at any job level in a specific industry.

  Farm magazines and service or professional magazines—such as those addressed to lawyers, doctors, nurses, teachers, and accountants—complete the print media category.
- **Out-of-home.** This group of media includes billboards and signs, as well as what is known as **transit advertising**—all the cards and signs you see on buses, trains, or subways and in airports, railroad stations, bus stops, and other such waiting places.

How much do you pay the media? That depends on two things: (1) the size (**space**) of your advertisement in a print or out-of-home medium or the length of **time** on television or radio and (2) the number of readers, viewers, or listeners who are expected to see or hear your ad. Each publication or broadcasting station develops its own **rate card,** based on these numbers. (See Chapters 8 and 9 for greater detail.) Salespeople from the media are glad to have a chance to go over their rates and the size of their circulation or audience with you. You may find that some rate cards are ironclad, while others are negotiable, depending on current market conditions for the medium and on the quantity of advertising you buy. Usually, you can get a frequency discount if you run a certain number of advertisements within a specified period.

If you hire an advertising agency, whom do you pay? You pay the agency. The agency pays the medium. Does this mean you pay more for your advertising? No. Traditionally, the media allowed their "agents" to keep 15 percent of the cost of any advertising they sold (this is the origin of the term *advertising agency*). If an advertiser, for example, bought $100 worth of newspaper space, the agency billed the advertiser for $100 but paid the newspaper $85, keeping $15 as its commission. The agency had to pay all its costs—salaries, overhead, and the like—and make its profit out of the 15 percent. For a hundred years or so, that was pretty much the standard in the business.

Times have changed. Giant agencies still keep the 15 percent commission rule in some cases. But this figure has eroded as media-buying services and agencies have been willing to work for smaller commissions. And smaller agencies, many of which come under the small-business heading themselves, have found that they simply cannot provide professional services and survive on 15 percent of the cost of local advertising or business-to-business advertising. As a result, today you find agencies large and small that operate on any of four different kinds of overall **compensation arrangements** with the advertisers who are their clients:

- *Commission arrangements.* (1) **Media commissions,** plus charges for materials and services provided for the client, plus charges for certain specified "inside" services. (2) Media commissions, plus charges for materials and services purchased, but with no charges for inside services. (3) Media commissions only.
- *Commission and fee arrangements.* (1) One of the three previous commission arrangements, plus an overall additional fee. (2) One of the three commission arrangements, but with a profit floor and a profit ceiling. (3) A minimum fee against which media commissions are credited.
- *Fixed fee.* An overall fee is agreed upon in advance.
- *Cost plus.* The overall cost of handling the business, calculated after the work is done.

Usually, the advertiser signs a contract or letter of agreement with the agency, specifying the compensation arrangement and including a clause that says the agreement may be canceled by either party upon due notice (usually 90 days, to allow time to complete any work in progress or to fulfill commitments to the media).

How about the **à la carte services?** How do you pay them? In most cases, you can expect to pay on a project-by-project basis. The service meets with you, gets an idea of what you want to do, studies your needs, then comes back with a quote for doing the particular job. Either with or without negotiation on the price, you agree on the job and the work proceeds. Or you may even get quotes, or bids, from two or three services and then choose the lowest price or the most promising plan. When the project has been completed, you and the à la carte service have no further obligations to one another—until you call them in to discuss another project. In sum, you are buying and paying for only those specific services that you want.

You Mean, There's More?

In very recent years, the advertising business has begun to include several ancillary categories of communication that help the selling of products and services either directly or indirectly. Known as integrated marketing communications, these are:

- **Direct response.** This category includes all the media in which the consumer buys directly from the manufacturer or wholesaler, rather than going to a store or other outlet. Direct mail (unfortunately referred to as "junk mail" by many) is one example. Others are mail order; cable television, with its shop-at-home channels; telemarketing, or selling over the telephone; and the very latest, advertising on computer networks.
- **Sales promotion.** Included under this heading is a wide variety of material, ranging from coupons and newspaper inserts to premiums and point-of-purchase displays, from exhibit booths at conventions and trade shows to contests and sweepstakes.
- **Public relations.** Many people confuse publicity with public relations. Publicity is but one aspect of the overall field that addresses the question of how your company is viewed by your public. This is the one area in which you cannot pay any medium to carry your message. Rather, you try to have yourself judged by what you do, not by what you say.

All three of these ancillary aspects of the advertising business are described in detail in Chapters 10, 11, and 12.

First Step: What Are the Tasks to Be Done?

Whether or not you hire an agency, buy à la carte services, or set up a full in-house advertising department, certain **tasks** must be performed in order to run an advertising program successfully. So before you start thinking about *who* does what, you must think about the *what,* what must be done to produce and place advertising. The tasks involved must be identified and defined. If you skip this step, you run the risk of not assigning important responsibilities or of duplicating assignments or of making assignments that are not appropriate—all of which can be costly in time, effort, and money. Fill in names or titles in the box on page 23 to assign tasks. You may find it more worthwhile to come back and fill in the table later, after you have completed reading this book. It is important at this point, however, to understand the different tasks involved in managing an advertising program.

This checklist will help you to see to whom you are assigning the responsibility for each task. By using this list, referring to it, and updating it regularly, you can keep track of all the functions that are part of your advertising program.

Summary

An advertiser is an individual or firm that pays for time or space in a medium of communication in order to reach an audience. Local businesses are responsible for nearly half of all advertising.

An advertising agency creates and places advertising on behalf of advertisers and handles other related tasks. The relationship of an agency to an advertiser is that of a partner rather than that of a vendor—that is, philosophically, not financially. The agency can provide a number of useful benefits to the advertiser. Two alternatives to using an agency's services are (1) buying à

TASK ASSIGNMENTS

Task	WHO DOES? We do	Agency does	Other does*
1. Marketing planning	________	________	________
2. Advertising budgeting	________	________	________
3. Strategic advertising planning	________	________	________
4. Creative planning—electronic	________	________	________
5. Creative planning—print	________	________	________
6. Creative planning—IMC**	________	________	________
7. Creative execution—electronic	________	________	________
8. Creative execution—print	________	________	________
9. Creative execution—IMC	________	________	________
10. Production—electronic	________	________	________
11. Production—print	________	________	________
12. Production—IMC**	________	________	________
13. Media planning—electronic	________	________	________
14. Media planning—print	________	________	________
15. Media execution—electronic	________	________	________
16. Media execution—print	________	________	________
17. Media performance measure	________	________	________
18. Market research—planning	________	________	________
19. Market research—execution	________	________	________
20. Advertising research—planning	________	________	________
21. Advertising research—execution	________	________	________
22. Budget control	________	________	________
23. Cost control—media	________	________	________
24. Cost control—electronic production	________	________	________
25. Cost control—print production	________	________	________
26. Cost control—IMC production	________	________	________
27. Cost control—agency compensation	________	________	________
28. Other (define)	________	________	________

* In the "Other does" column, list the organization (such as an à la carte service) or individual (or position title) responsible for performing the task.

**IMC = Integrated Marketing Communications.

Source: Charles B. Jones. *Advertising Services: Full-Service Agency, A La Carte, Or In-House* New York: Association of National Advertisers, Inc., copyright 1991; Reprinted with permission.

la carte services and (2) handling the advertising program entirely in-house.

The media that accept payment for carrying advertising messages include electronic (broadcast television and radio, cable television), print (newspapers, magazines), and out-of-home (billboards and signs, transit). How much you pay the media depends on the size or length of time of your advertising message and on the size of the audience receiving your message.

The compensation arrangement for an agency's services may take any of several forms, including a commission to the agency from the medium, a fee arrangement, a cost-plus arrangement, or some combination of two or more of these. A la carte services are usually assigned and paid for on a project-by-project basis.

In addition to the traditional media, the advertising business today includes integrated marketing communications, ranging from direct response media to sales promotion to public relations.

To establish a foundation for handling your advertising program, it is important to review all tasks to be done and assign them to specific individuals or to an agency, if one is being used.

CHAPTER THREE

The Marketing Plan

KEY TERMS

advertising plan
advertising-to-sales ratio
awareness
benefit
claims
competitive advantages
creative plan
creative strategy
crossover marketing
demographic characteristics
image
integrated marketing
management summary
media flowchart
media plan
niche marketing
positioning
problems and opportunities
production
psychographics
relationship marketing
research
share of the market
share of voice
situation analysis
target marketing
value added

Many small businesses run haphazard advertising campaigns. They spend money unnecessarily. They try to save just where they should be spending: on professional services and quality work. They move too fast, jumping into media because convincing salespeople come around. How does this happen? Usually because they don't ask themselves tough questions about who their customers are, or might be, and how to reach them. They don't stop to think that advertising money is invested for a specific reason, with the expectation of a specific result, and that—as when making any investment—they must know what they expect the result to be.

Whatever Your Size, You Need a Marketing Plan

What such businesses really need, whether they realize it or not, is a marketing plan. It asks the tough questions. And answers them. Yet owners of small businesses think they don't have time to prepare marketing plans. Or they think a formal plan will be a burden. Or they think following one takes too much time. A marketing plan? they say, that's for the big boys, the giant corporations. But the fact is that if you cannot put a marketing plan in writing, you probably are running your business without any plan at all. And that is not healthy.

Putting your marketing plan in writing helps you organize your thinking. It also cuts down on misunderstandings among your staff. A marketing plan establishes what you want to do and how you expect to do it, so others will have a clear picture of your intentions, even if you are not there. In fact, a good plan is one that someone from outside, who doesn't know your business, can read and understand.

There are good practical reasons for working up your marketing plan, too. Many banks and other lending institutions will want to see a marketing plan before making a loan. If they don't, they should—for their own protection. Developing a marketing plan also helps you and your people be innovative, to think up new ideas. It gives you a handle on what costs to expect and be ready for. It gives you insight into the future, helping you see problems and opportunities. It helps you manage your time and put your priorities in order.

Think About Your Marketing

Before you sit down to write your marketing plan, think about several types of marketing that have become fundamental to retailing in recent years. They are not, however, exclusive to retailing. If you are selling business-to-business, you can find them equally useful.

- **Target marketing.** If you think there is still such a thing as an average customer, you are sadly behind the times. There are only individuals, each of whom considers almost any purchase with great care. No two customers have quite the same **demographic characteristics**—age, sex, income, education, marital status, number of children, street address, or neighborhood. With today's databases, from zip codes to checkout scanners and UPC codes, it is possible to know exactly who your customers are and to pull together into key groups data on those customers who are most alike. You can pinpoint members of those groups that have the buying habits you are most interested in, count them, identify them by name and address, and predict the buying patterns that are to be expected. Target marketing means that you aim an attractive, believable message at the most likely customer through the most appropriate medium at the time when your message is most likely to succeed.
- **Relationship marketing.** Something else has changed. Adversarial marketing, in which each person at each stage of the business exchange was out to best everyone else, with no thought to the long term, has evolved into relationship marketing—an effort to build lasting associations among employees, suppliers, and customers. Why? Studies have shown that it costs you five times as much to win a new customer for your product or service as it does to sell to a previous customer. Treating a customer as a good relation brings back the satisfied customer again and again.

Thinking about relationship marketing can help you get away from "sale" marketing, in which you depend on price to move your merchandise. Merchandise offered at a fair price, but not necessarily the lowest price, that comes with reliable service and that is targeted to a key group can bring customers to you.

- **Crossover marketing.** Suppose you're running a video rental store. A few doors away in your shopping center is a pizza parlor. You make a deal with the pizza parlor: With every take-home pizza, the parlor offers a coupon good for a discount at your video store. And at your video store, every tape rental includes a coupon providing a discount on a take-home pizza. Call it customer sharing. You can apply the crossover idea in countless ways.
- **Integrated marketing.** More about this broad subject in Part IV, but remember it now as a key element in your marketing plan. It involves making sure all your messages to your customers build on one another, whether these messages are in paid media advertising, sales promotion, or public relations.
- **Niche marketing.** This is like target marketing, but thinking about the word *niche* will help you decide whether you are selling a product that appeals to such a small market that the big companies don't even consider you competition. That's what happened to Harry Heller. He produced a line of Harry's Premium Snacks, which were made with the best oils and which were hand-cooked. His snacks cost more to make and distribute than typical Frito-Lay snacks, but Harry knew that specialty and health-food stores needed high-quality snack foods for their customers. So he set a policy: His products would not be sold in the snack aisles of supermarkets, and he would set fair prices, which would cover costs and profits and reflect the quality of the product. Introduced in 1987, Harry's Premium Snacks has doubled its sales every year.

As you think about the different types of marketing, consider this: The Dun & Bradstreet study mentioned at the beginning of Chapter 1 found that small businesses fall into one of five categories:

- Twenty-five percent are *decliners.* These are older companies fighting to survive.
- Ten percent are *stragglers.* They don't use computers. They have no strong marketing direction.
- Seventeen percent are *self-sufficient expanders.* They are do-it-yourselfers. No outside services for them.
- Twenty-three percent are *successful entrepreneurs.* These are local companies whose owners make decisions unilaterally.
- Twenty-five percent are *pacesetters.* These are the marketing-oriented ones. They are the innovators. They are growing.

Which one of these describes you and your business?

First Things First: Analyze Your Market

Now carry your thinking a couple of steps further. Exactly who is your target market, and what are your objectives for that group? Who would you like your customers to be? Why do people buy, or don't buy, your products?

With today's databases, you can zero in on your customer base. Marketing professors have always said that 20 percent of a small business's customers account for 80 percent of its sales. But who are the 20 percent? If you are keeping good records, you know who buys how much and how often. One menswear store figured out that only 1.5 percent of its customers accounted for 11 percent of its sales.

And don't forget to analyze inactive customers, those who have bought from you but have drifted away. Your database program can identify them, so you can target them as well as your active customers in your marketing plan.

If you are a retailer and you are like most, your primary objective in developing your marketing plan is to build traffic. You want to get people into the store, whether they are regular customers, inactive customers, or first-time customers.

You should have a second objective that is almost, if not equally, as important: to build your store's **image,** its personality. Your store's personality is determined by what the store looks like, what kind of merchandise it carries, the design of all its communications, even the personalities of the people behind the counter. From cash register tapes to shopping bags to advertising itself, all things connected with your store should reflect the correct image. Ideally, the real or potential customer should be able to identify your store from that "look," without even seeing your store's name. In effect, your store's "look" is selecting your customers.

Another reason you need to think hard about your marketing situation before you draw up your marketing plan: Advertising is not a panacea. It is not simple. It is not a ready-made solution to all your business problems. That's why setting objectives is important. You must know precisely what you need to achieve, rather than saying, Business is slow, maybe some ads will help.

The Other Side of the Scrimmage Line: The Competition

In forming your marketing plan, don't think only about yourself. Think about your competition. Who or what are your competitors? Can you pinpoint their weaknesses and strengths? Try to see where they are vulnerable. Figure out what their **share of the market** is. And how much they are spending on advertising. Think about their customers. Are they the same as yours? If so, how come they are not *your* customers? What makes your competitors different from you?

If your competition is selling the same merchandise you are, and if the price is about the same, what makes you different? What makes your store the better place to go? The most promising answer is service. People look for top-notch service today, and usually it is not easy to find. Are your competitors earning the loyalty of customers by offering a wider variety of styles and sizes, more courteous and personalized service, faster response on special orders?

Experts in the psychology of business say that competition for sales takes four forms or stages. To understand these, imagine that you are running a paint store. You are competing for your potential customer's business in four basic areas:

- *Want.* Among all the wants that have surfaced in your customer's mind on a

Saturday morning is the urge to improve the appearance of a room in his or her home. This want has competed with and won out over all others, such as mowing the lawn, tending the garden, playing golf, going swimming, whatever.

- *Generic.* This category of competition has narrowed your customer's thinking down to fresh paint. Competing against the idea of washing the walls and woodwork or wallpapering the room, the generic idea of painting has won.
- *Form.* Now the competition is between products that can solve the problem. In this case, it is between water-based and oil-based paints and between flat, semigloss, and gloss finishes. Not only that, but all the colors in the rainbow are in competition with one another. Unlike the first two forms of competition, this one will be played out in the paint stores.
- *Brand.* Now it is Sherwin-Williams versus Pratt & Lambert versus Benjamin Moore versus Devoe versus Pittsburgh. This brand-name competition is the one everybody knows about. It goes on all the time between manufacturers in their national advertising. But usually the game is won or lost in the paint store.

This four-step sequence is the same, whether the customer is in the market for furniture, skis, banking services, automobiles, men's shirts, personal computers, carpet cleaning, linens, travel services, lawn mowers, or anything else. It is the competitive process that brings the customer to your business or takes the customer elsewhere. In most cases, you get the opportunity to influence the outcome of the competition only in stages 3 and 4. Your marketing plan must show how you are going to exert your influence in those stages.

How Are You Different? Positioning

How you *position* your business can make the difference between whether the customer comes to you or goes somewhere else. To beat out the competition, there must be some difference between your product or service and theirs that your target audience can easily perceive. How is your product or service different? How is your store different? If you are running the paint store, are you the only store around that has a computerized color-matching system, so you can custom-blend paints to match your customers' decors? Or do you have a talented decorator on staff who can offer the professional advice your competition can't? If you are a car dealer, do you have a salesman who says to customers, "Whenever you need to bring your new car here for servicing, just give me a call. I'll pick it up first thing in the morning and leave you a loaner to use until I bring your car back"? If you are selling men's shirts, can you promise customers they will find "tall guy" sizes that don't pull out at the waist in everything from button-down-collar 100 percent cotton oxford-cloth dress shirts to wash-and-wear short-sleeved crinkly seersuckers, so you can position your haberdashery as "the tall guys' store"? Or, if you're selling sportswear to women, can you claim to be "the big store for the petite lady"? If yours is one of the thousands of American communities that is seeing rapid ethnic change, can you tell your customers that you have salespeople ready, willing, and able to speak their language? All of these are examples of **positioning** that can help you win out over your competition.

Who's Who and Where Are They? Psychographics and Demographics

As you think about and analyze the customers in your target market, you will be looking at what they have in common. You can organize them (or the data about them) in several ways:

- *By geography. Where* is your product or service most likely to be used? Big cities? Small towns? In warm climates? Cold climates? If you want to move your inventory of self-propelled lawn mowers, for example, your target audience is more likely to be people who live on hillsides than those whose lawns are flat and level. What geographical aspects categorize *your* target audience?
- *By demography.* Here you're thinking about age, sex, income, education, marital status, family size, owning a home versus renting. Which of the variables in all these characteristics do certain of your customers (or potential customers, don't forget) have in common? When you put the data together, useful information should emerge. Say you're running a gourmet restaurant. The number of moderate-income families with at least four kids in your marketing area will not be nearly as important for advertising purposes as the number of high-income childless or empty-nest couples. But if you are running a pizza parlor, you want to identify and quantify that large-family, moderate-income group.
- *By psychography.* What goes on inside your customer's head is another consideration. How your advertising appeals to or influences a bookkeeper may be very different from how it affects a schoolteacher or a newspaper reporter or a doctor or nurse. Most people know their own life-styles. They know where they stand (or sit) in social groups. They perceive whether advertising is addressed to them. Will yours get through to them?
- *By media use.* It doesn't really matter which media *you* want to place your advertising in. What counts is what television, newspapers, magazines, radio, and out-of-home media your target market—your customers, past, present, and future—watch, read, listen to, and see. And *when* they read, watch, listen, and see.
- *By product use.* If someone who is seeing or hearing your advertising simply has no use for your product or service, you don't have much chance of making a sale, no matter how right your advertising is in all other respects. So when you are planning, you need to figure out how many *users* are in your target group and how much of your product or service they use and how often.

Just What's in a Marketing Plan, Anyway?

The elements of a marketing plan fall into two broad areas: first, the gathering of everything you know about your product or service and second, a plan for attaining the objectives that you set. Important: Put both of these down on paper so you can review, revise, and discuss them with your people, and so you can update them on a regular basis. Here's what to include.

1. Situation Analysis

This is your foundation. Accurately, realistically, and honestly write down everything factual that you know or can find out about your situation. Be thorough and try to be concise. Include facts on the following:

- *Your product or service.* Its distinctive features, any advantages it has over the competition's, and any advantages the competition's enjoys.
- *Your marketplace.* Total sales of all who are competing and the market share of each competitor. Anticipated growth of the market for the next year and next five years.
- *Distribution.* How your product moves to how many stores, and what types of stores these are.
- *Pricing.* What you are charging today. What have you been charging for the past five years? What will you for the coming year? For the next five years?
- *Advertising and promotion.* What is your **share of voice?** Of all the dollars spent by you and your competitors for advertising and promotion, what percentage do *you* spend? This year? Past five years? Next five?
- *Customers or consumers.* Who buys the product or service, what makes them decide to buy it, what do they like or not like about it?
- *Your customers.* The same questions: Who buys? Why? What do they think of it?

2. Problems and Opportunities

Now start analyzing. Look over your situation analysis. What problems do you see in the characteristics of your product or service, in distribution, in pricing, in each of the situation categories? Write them down.

A problem is likely to present an opportunity. A poor share of market is a problem you can tackle, for example, by increasing your share of voice. But if your situation analysis reveals that your share of voice is already larger than your share of market, but it is not increasing your share of market, your analysis will have revealed a different problem: Something is wrong with your advertising and promotion program. It is not working.

The most important thing is to identify problems and start doing something about them. Any problem you recognize but ignore is an opportunity for your competitors. Any problem that you can solve is an opportunity for you.

What if you just cannot find a solution to a clearly evident problem? Think **research.** You can set up a research plan to chase down the solution to almost any problem you identify. Two warnings, however: First, remember that research is for professionals. Bring in competent consultants. Second, watch the cost. If the price of research is greater than 5 percent of the sales you expect, it is too high.

3. Goals or Objectives

Most marketing-plan goals are expressed in dollars. What sales revenue do you expect for the fiscal year? What's the percentage change from the preceding year?

How about profit before taxes, and its change from last year? Think long-range, too—five years ahead and five years back—to give a complete picture.

Your objective may also be expressed in share of market. What percentage of the total market for the product or service is yours right now? What percent are you shooting for, in one year or in five years?

You may have a secondary goal that you want to express, such as improving the image of your company or generating **awareness** of it (if, for instance, you are expanding into new territory or your situation analysis shows that you are not very well known where you already are). Or you may want to build up store traffic or inquiries. Warning: Don't pile up too many objectives. One primary goal with a couple of secondaries will give you plenty to cope with.

4. Advertising Plan

Now you are getting into communication. This is the first of several tactical plans you will put into your overall marketing plan. It is the "what we must do" stage, but it is not yet the "how we will do it" stage.

Put down the "what we must do" on paper in several steps:

- *Define the problem.* Identify the problem you want advertising to solve, based on conclusions from your situation analysis. Is it your store's, or your product's, overall image? An incorrect opinion people have? A misperception about why your price is higher than the customer expects? A manufacturing or distribution problem that limits availability?
- *Identify the opportunities.* What opportunities can you produce from the problem? Does your pricing policy translate into a *value* the customer can enjoy? Saturn automobile made its no-haggling price policy a part of the car's value. Does limited availability make the product fashionable or irresistible?
- *State the objectives.* What do you want advertising to achieve? These may include a rehash of your overall marketing-plan objectives but with refinements. Example: You may say the objective is to "increase sales," as you did in the earlier marketing objective, but now you add "by getting new users to try" the product or service. Or you may have other possible refinements: "by getting current users to use it more frequently" or "by getting current users to try new uses for it." Put it all in a time frame: Include the date or dates by which you want the objectives to be attained.
- *Define your target audience.* Figure out whom it is important to talk to. Maybe you have two or three target audiences. Rank them in order of preference, determining what percentage of the total users, or total market, are in each target audience.

This is where you pull in the demographic, geographic, and psychographic information from your situation analysis. Describe the audience you want to reach in terms of each of these "graphic" aspects. Is it women aged 22 to 40 who work full-time, have two or more preschool and school-age children, drive the second car in the family, have a total family income of about $42,000 a year, and do most of the household shopping on Thursday evening between 7 and 9? Is it office managers who need spreadsheet and word-processing programming that ties together a local area network of nine personal computers, three printers, and a file server?

- *Describe the advantages.* What advantages does your product or service offer over its competition? List them thoughtfully in order of importance to the buyer (not in order of importance to you, which may be quite different). Advantages can range from price to quality, from a one-year (or longer) guarantee to round-the-clock service, from the variety of styles and colors offered to the time saved by using yours.

  Here's one way to set up a clear analysis of your **competitive advantages** and disadvantages. Mark four columns on a page. Head the first one "Generic," the second "Ours," the third "Competitor 1," and the fourth "Competitor 2." Under Generic, list the features that any buyer is looking for when in the market for the generic product or service. Rank these features by how important you think they are to the buyer. Now, beside each feature on the generic list, fill in a comment that tells how you and each of your two most worrisome competitors measure up. As strengths and weaknesses appear, you will soon be able to see where attention must be paid.

  Here's another competitive advantage to look for. Some advertising people call it **value added.** Does your product, service, or store offer some feature that directly meets a customer need and that your competitors do not offer? Are you open longer hours? Do you offer a wider selection? Maintain larger inventory? Give a senior discount or early-bird special on more days? What value-added components can you come up with that will help your business to stand out from your competitors?

- *Plot the positioning you want.* Write down a brief description of how you want your customers to think of your store or product or service: As bright, trendy, upscale, selling only the best at top prices? As first to introduce the latest? As rock-bottom lowest-priced? Some companies position themselves by putting the word *budget* in their company names. You know immediately what competitive advantage they are offering.

- *Build in a budget figure.* Note how much was budgeted for advertising last year. List the reasons for (1) any change upward or downward or (2) no change. (For details on how to figure out how much money you should allocate to advertising, see the next section, Where Do You Get the Money for Advertising?)

5. Creative Plan

This is your second plan-within-the-plan. Now you are into "how we will do it." You are planning how you will communicate with the readers and listeners and viewers you most want to reach. Your creative plan should include several sections:

- *Creative strategy.* Describe how the advertising you produce will relate to the marketing objectives you have set up. If your marketing objective is "to increase sales by getting new users to try" or "by getting customers to use more," your creative strategy may say your advertising will "demonstrate the wide variety of uses" for your product or service. When Scotch-brand cellophane tape was introduced many years ago, the 3M Company spent several years and millions of dollars showing thousands of uses for it.

A business-to-business creative strategy can be quite similar. The R.T. Vanderbilt Company of Norwalk, Connecticut, is unknown to the consumer. It makes or processes a wide variety of ingredient products used in manufacturing cosmetics, paper, paint, and rubber products. For many years the consistent creative strategy of its advertising has been to provide research and development people in those industries with new and improved formulas that call for Vanderbilt ingredients.

- *Creative target.* Now you describe the people to whom you are directing your advertising. Your description here is more psychographic than demographic: Maybe you want sports nuts or theater buffs or den mothers or vegetable gardeners or chemists or electrical engineers or computer programmers to pay attention. Whatever your target or targets, get a brief description down on paper.
- *Creative rationale.* Now explain why you think your advertising is going to work. Can you say, "Cosmetologists will read our ads and try our formula because they are trying to find eye shadow that will last 18 hours without touch-up"? Or, "By offering a senior discount from opening until noon on Monday through Wednesday, we can build traffic at our slowest times because senior citizens want discounts and are free to shop in the morning."
- *Creative execution.* Here you describe how your advertising will approach its audience. For example, if you are selling fashions or furniture or decoration or carpet cleaning, you may be planning to appeal to peoples' self-esteem. If you are selling alarm systems or fire extinguishers, the appeal is to fear and the need for security. If price and cost are the basic message, you are appealing to the customer's sense of value and economy. If the focus is quick-and-easy to use, your appeal is convenience. All such approaches are basically psychological ones.

You can build approaches on other bases. One is by making **claims** about your product or service. "Contains less fat, "fewer calories," "more pepperminty taste," and "dries ready to rehang your pictures in 10 minutes" are all claims for several different products. Important: If you go this route, you have to be extra careful that your advertising promises a **benefit** to its audience. "Paint at 4, party at 5" offers a benefit to the buyer that is backed up by the quick-drying claim. Always use a claim not to sell but to back up a benefit that sells. And always try to get your reader's or listener's imagination involved. If the message said only "Dries in 10 minutes," it wouldn't give the audience a way to imagine the benefits of this quick drying. "Dries ready to rehang your pictures in 10 minutes" puts the imagination to work.

Here you may want to include some samples of your advertising, if some has already been produced or is in the rough conceptual stage.

- *Creative research.* You may or may not plan some research connected with your creative work (see also Chapter 5). If you do, include it here in the creative plan. For instance, if the objective of your advertising is to increase awareness of your store or product or service, you will need to do a study before the advertising starts to appear to establish how well known you are. Otherwise, how can you measure an increase? Then, periodic follow-up studies will tell you whether, and to what extent, your advertising has increased awareness.

  If you are studying whether readers recall your advertising (again, see Chapter 5), plans for such studies should be noted.

- *Creative budget.* What's all the creative work going to cost? Not the cost of the media in which you place the advertising (you'll get to that in the media plan section of your marketing plan), but just the cost of the creative work: getting copy written, advertisements laid out, negatives and four-color plates made for printing, radio and television commercials produced, and the talent paid? Compile a total **production** cost and add at least 10 percent for contingencies you haven't thought of or cannot foresee.

- *Production timetable.* This tells what must be done by when. Where to begin? Begin at the end. Figure out exactly when you want your advertising to appear. That's the ultimate end date. Now work backward. For your advertising to appear in a certain issue of a publication or on the air on a certain date, how many days or weeks before that must negatives or plates or videotape or audiotape be delivered to the publisher or broadcaster? To make *that* date, how many days or weeks (or even months) earlier must production start? And to meet *that* deadline, how far ahead must someone be writing the copy and designing the ad layout or the television storyboard that will guide production? *And* to be ready to start writing and designing, how much earlier must a writer and art director (see Chapter 4) sit down with you or your advertising or marketing director to talk about what is going to be advertised?

  All those who are or expect to be involved, media salespeople, production people, copywriters, art directors, can help pull the timetable or schedule together. A good idea: Give your computer the responsibility for putting all this information into a spreadsheet or time line that you can attach, as an exhibit, to this section of the creative plan.

6. Media Plan

Here comes your third plan-within-the-plan. It details how your advertising messages are going to reach the audience you want. (You may find it helpful to look ahead to Part III.) Key sections to include:

- *Media strategy.* This time, you are relating the purchase of media to your overall marketing objectives. It may seem obvious, but it is important to state it. If, for example, your marketing objective is to attract customers to your store from a wider radius than in the past, the media strategy may be as simple as buying space in newspapers and time on local radio stations in those cities and towns you expect to draw customers from. If your marketing objective is to sell your business-to-business product or service to industries that have not used it before, your media strategy is to buy space in publications read by executives in those industries.

- *Media objective or target.* Here you are talking demographics as well as psychographics. You are really describing your target audience again but in terms of media: Mechanical engineers aged 35 to 50 with B.S. degrees who are in decision-making management positions in plants in the New England states and who read such publications as *American Machinist.* Or upscale married adults aged 25 to 60 who live or travel in the mountain region from Maryland to Georgia and who read such publications as *Blue Ridge Country.* Or unmarried white-collar workers aged 22 to 32 who are not yet middle managers and who—as they commute by car 10 to 40 minutes each weekday morning and evening—listen to top-40 country-and-western radio. The more of that kind of description you can provide, the better. It will help you, or your media person, select the most appropriate media for your advertising message and dollars.
- *Media research.* If the media that keep pounding on your door and pitching for your business can provide dependable research, include it here. Their data should be able to tell demographically, geographically, and psychographically who reads their publications, sees and hears their broadcasts or cablecasts, or passes by their out-of-home postings. Including their research will help to rationalize your media-buying decisions.
- *Media execution.* Now comes the nitty-gritty. Which media are recommended by this plan? Set up a section for each medium—newspapers, magazines, radio, television broadcast, television cablecast, out-of-home—and list within each the specific publications or stations or postings to be bought. To show just what you are getting for your money, include for each the gross rating points, the reach and average frequency expected, and the budget expenditure in dollars.

  A valuable addition to this section is a list of media that are *not* recommended, with reasons why. This will help to answer questions now as well as to remind you of media to be considered again next time your marketing plan is reviewed.
- *Media flowchart.* Set up a spreadsheet that looks ahead a full year, showing how much you will be spending in each quarter and in each medium. It should also show the scheduling of print advertisements and of commercials week by week. The **media flowchart** becomes the detailed graphic illustration of your media plan.

7. Integrated Marketing Communications

This is yet another plan-within-the-plan. (See Part IV for more information on integrated marketing communications.) For each of three areas—sales promotion, direct response, and public relations—follow the sequence you have now so well established, writing down clear and simple objectives, the strategies for achieving them, the target audiences to be addressed, your explanation of how the strategies will affect the audiences, sample executions for each type of communication, any pertinent research that can measure results, a budget (including production, shipping, and postage) and a timetable. Other points for you to consider in these three areas:

- *Sales promotion.* Objectives and strategies for sales promotion may be addressed both to the trade and to the consumer or to business-to-business customers. Are you determined to stimulate immediate sales to solve an overstock problem? Do you want to introduce a new product quickly? Think a contest or sweepstakes will get people involved? Willing to give a rebate or refund on the purchase price? Ready to distribute coupons through the mail or in freestanding inserts in publications? Need eye-catching displays at the point of purchase, descriptive pamphlets for countertops, brochures to answer inquiries? Headed for an annual trade show or convention that calls for an exhibit booth? These are typical situations you might address in the sales promotion plan within your marketing plan. There are countless others. Don't forget to include promotional materials or events—contests and incentives—for your own salespeople.
- *Direct response.* Here you describe any plans you have for selling by mail order or direct mail. (In mail order, the buyer orders from you by mail after seeing your advertising in any medium; in direct mail, the buyer receives advertising from you by mail and responds by mail or by telephone or fax). Or you may be selling directly on television and have phone and fax orders coming in. Your plan may also call for telemarketing, direct promotion and selling to customers by telephone.
- *Public relations.* Having set objectives, described target audiences, and established budget needs, your public relations plan will detail how you expect to deal with the media (the editorial or journalistic side of media) when you are putting on special events (your anniversary celebration, open house, plant dedication), how you will handle employee relations (internal newsletters, audiovisual training materials) and community relations (sponsoring Little League teams; participating in parades, seminars; speaking at service club luncheons and dinners). Don't forget an important contingency: Your plan should include standby preparations for the inevitable crisis—fire or accident or other disaster, embezzlement by an employee, a major failure of your product or service, or whatever could give your business bad publicity or hamper your service to customers.

8. Management Summary

At this point, you can pull together an executive summary that condenses your entire marketing plan. Put it at the beginning of the plan, before all the detailed information, so that a stranger can read the few paragraphs (totaling not more than two pages) and get an overview of the entire plan.

Include what may seem obvious: full names of your products or services and brief descriptions of the markets in which you are selling them. Talk total revenue goals as well as profit goals, including percent of change over last year. Explain your primary objective (and maybe a secondary objective if it is essential to your summary) and your rationale for expecting to achieve it. Review your strategy for reaching the objective, but don't go into the details of how you will execute the strategy. Summarize your situation analysis, hitting the key facts. And summarize your major recommendations on creative work and media. Conclude with overall budget figures, including total costs or costs for the major areas (media, production, and integrated marketing communications), but don't break down the costs into more specific detail here. Finally, let the reader in on key dates and deadlines and the next steps to be taken.

Where Do You Get The Money for Advertising?

Some small businesses fall into the habit of letting their advertising budgets just happen. One day a salesperson from the local newspaper comes into the store and talks about a special back-to-school or June-wedding supplement you'd be crazy not to be in. Another day some awfully nice person from the community theater group arrives to tell you the program for next year's three-show season is about to go to press. Or a salesperson from a magazine in your industry arrives at your plant to show you the dummy of the biggest single-subject issue they've ever published, one that's sure to be kept right on key decision makers' desks for a year or more.

Some small-business advertisers budget a lump sum based on their experience over several years of meeting the demands of such people, some of whom are superb at selling and some of whom simply pluck at the heartstrings.

Your advertising budget has to be based on something—unless you like to pick numbers out of the air. You may use any of several methods to arrive at an overall dollar figure. The most popular method, used by some two-thirds of local as well as industrial advertisers, is the percentage-of-sales method. But many simply use their judgment, spending whatever they can afford or whatever their competitors seem to be spending (if they can match it.) The following methods are commonly used.

Advertising-to-Sales Ratio

Here you set up a percentage that represents the ratio of advertising dollars to sales dollars you expect for the coming year. If you want to increase sales over this year, you must plan to increase the ratio. To see where your ratio is, or has been up to now, take your past advertising dollars (either this year's or an average of the past several years') and divide it by your sales (also current or an average of past sales). This will give you your present percentage of sales.

What advertising-to-sales ratio will be

the right one for your business? An annual study by Schonfeld & Associates, Inc., (see box page 40-41) can give you some clues. Apparel and accessory stores spend 2.2 percent of their sales dollars on advertising; building material, hardware, and gardening retailers, 3.3 percent; cutlery, hand tools, and general hardware, 10.2; eating places, 3.2; furniture stores, 6.4; retail stores in general, 4.6. If you're making sugar and confectionery products, your ratio may be as high as 12.7 percent, and if you are in the business of manufacturing games, toys (except dolls), and children's vehicles, it may be even higher—16.4 percent. On the other hand, if you're selling financial services, you may find it as low as .9 percent. Studying this list can give you insight into what goes on in your line of business.

Advertising Share of Voice

To use this method, you need to know your share of market and your share of voice. If you are spending 20 percent of the total advertising dollars being spent in your market, you have a 20 percent share of voice. If your share of the total market is 15 percent, and if you continue to spend at the 20 percent share-of-voice ratio, your share of market should rise, provided you are spending your money on effective advertising. However, if your share of market is 20 percent and you spend at a share-of-voice ratio of 15 percent, your share of market is likely to go down—even if you are producing good advertising. Why? Because you are asking for a smaller share of the consumer's mind than your present share of market. You are waving bye-bye.

Advertising Objective

This method begins with a question: What will it cost to attain our advertising objective? Suppose your objective is to make a certain percentage of your potential market aware of your store or product or service. You have to determine what it will cost to buy the media and produce the advertising to reach that percentage of people. This method may be your best choice in either of two situations: if you cannot obtain useful figures on share of voice or share of market or if your objective is to improve the image of your firm or store or to increase awareness of it, neither of which is a direct sales objective.

Watch the Pitfalls

Don't let your marketing plan fall into the quantity-over-quality trap. If your advertising budget is small, you may feel a great temptation to create and run many inexpensive small ads. But for the same amount of money, you can run a few good-quality, good-sized ads that make you look good, instead of a large number of small and cheap ads that make *you* look small and cheap.

Don't forget that advertising is only one part of your total marketing mix. All the other parts, from your product and its packaging and pricing to its promotion, are just as important. Advertising cannot solve all your problems.

Probably the most important thing to keep in mind about your marketing plan is that it is not set in concrete. It is a road map. It is always subject to change and

ADVERTISING AS A PERCENTAGE OF SALES

The 200 industries listed are those with the largest dollar volumes of advertising based on estimated 1994 spending.

Industry	Ad $ as % Sales
Abrasine, asbestos, Misc Minrl	1.1
Adhesives and sealants	4.8
Agriculture chemicals	1.3
Agriculture Production—crops	2.3
Air cond, heating, refrig eq	1.5
Air courier services	1.4
Air transport, scheduled	1.4
Apparel and other finished pds	5.6
Apparel and accessory stores	2.2
Auto and home supply stores	0.9
Auto rent and lease, no drivers	2.4
Bakery products	9.9
Beverages	7.5
Biological pds, ex diagnstics	1.3
Blank books, binders, bookbind	3.5
Bldg matl, hardwr, garden-retl	3.3
Books: pubg, pubg and printing	3.3
Brdwoven fabric mill, cotton	4.0
Btld and can soft drinks, water	2.7
Cable and other pay TV svcs	1.1
Calculate, acct mach, ex comp	1.8
Can fruit, veg, presrv, jam, jel	0.8
Can, frozn presrv fruit and veg	7.1
Carpets and rugs	2.4
Catalog, mail-order houses	6.8
Chemicals and allied pds-whsl	3.6
Chemicals and allied prods	2.8
Cigarettes	4.4
Cmp and cmp software stores	1.5
Cmp integrated sys design	1.5
Cmp processing, data prep svc	1.4
Communications equip, nec	1.5
Computer and office equipment	1.2
Computer communication equip	1.9
Computer peripheral eq, nec	2.8
Computer storage devices	0.8
Computers and software-whsl	0.5
Consruction machinery and eq	0.2
Convrt papr, paprbrd, ex boxes	5.8
Cutlery, hand tools, gen hrdwr	10.2
Dairy products	1.4
Dental equipment and supplies	2.0
Department stores	2.6
Dolls and stuffed toys	15.1
Drug and proprietary stores	1.4
Eating places	3.2
Educational services	6.5
Elec meas and test instruments	2.7
Electr, oth elec eq, ex cmp	2.4
Electric housewares and fans	5.1
Electric lighting, wiring eq	1.7
Electrical indl apparatus	2.3
Electromedical apparatus	1.0
Electronic comp, accessories	3.0
Electronic components, nec	0.8
Elecronic computers	1.7
Electronic parts, eq-whsl, nec	2.9
Engines and turbines	1.8
Engr, acc, resh, mgmt, rel svcs	0.7
Fabricated rubber pds, nec	1.5
Family clothing stores	2.5
Farm machinery and equipment	1.2
Finance-services	0.9
Food and kindred products	6.3
Food stores	4.2
Footwear, except rubber	3.8
Functions rel to dep bke, nec	11.5
Furniture stores	6.4
Games, toys, chld veh, ex dolls	16.4
Gen med and surgical hospitals	0.8
General indl mach and eq, nec	0.7
General industrial mach and eq	2.2
Glass, glasswr-pressed, blown	1.1
Grain mill products	9.1
Greeting cards	4.9
Groceries and related pds-whsl	2.0
Grocery stores	1.1
Guided missiles and space vehc	0.4
Hardwr, plumb, heat eq-whsl	2.3
Help supply services	1.0
Hobby, toy, and game shops	1.5
Home furniture and equip store	2.9
Hospital and medical svc plans	0.9
Hospitals	4.2
Hotels, motels, tourist courts	3.6
Household appliances	3.0
Household audio and video eq	3.6
Household furniture	4.6
Ice cream and frozen desserts	3.6
In vitro, in vivo diagnostics	2.1
indl coml fans, blowrs, oth eq	4.1
Indl trucks, tractors, trailrs	1.0
Industrial measurement instr	0.8
Industrial organic chemicals	0.8
Ins agents, brokers and service	1.1
Investment advice	7.3
Jewelry stores	4.3
Jewelry, precious metal	3.0

Industry	Ad $ as % Sales
Knit outerwear mills	2.8
Knitting mills	3.0
Lab analytical instruments	1.8
Lumber and oth bldg matl-retl	1.1
Lumber and wood pds, ex furn	0.2
Magnetc, optic recording mediatl	3.0
Malt beverages	5.5
Management services	1.5
Meas and controlling dev, nec	1.8
Meat packing plants	6.0
Membership sport and rec clubs	6.5
Men, yth, boys frnsh, wrk clthg	3.6
Metal forgings and stampings	0.9
Metalworking machinery and eq	3.1
Millwork, veneer, plywood	1.7
Misc amusement and rec service	2.6
Misc business services	3.9
Misc chemical products	7.2
Misc durable goods-whsl	2.0
Misc elec machy, eq, supplies	1.5
Misc fabricated metal prods	0.7
Misc food preps, kindred pds	2.9
Misc general mdse stores	3.6
Misc manufacturng industries	2.3
Misc nondurable goods-whsl	3.2
Misc plastics products	2.1
Misc shopping goods stores	2.2
Misc transportation equip	4.7
Miscellaneous retail	1.8
Mortgage bankers and loan corr	2.2
Motion pic, videotapt prodtn	12.4
Motion pict, videotape distr	6.3
Motion picture theaters	3.1
Motor vehicle part, accessory	0.8
Motor vehicles and car bodies	2.7
Motorcycles, bicycles and parts	1.2
Newspaper:pubg, pubg and print	3.4
Office machines, nec	1.2
Offices of medical doctors	1.4
Operative builders	1.1
Operators-nonres bldgs	1.6
Ophthalmic goods	8.4
Ortho, prosth, surg appl, suqly	2.1
Paints, varnishes, lacquers	2.7
Paper and paper products-whsl	1.6
Paper mills	3.0
Patent owners and lessors	4.3
Pens, pencils, oth office matl	4.7
Perfume, cosmetic, toilet prep	8.8
Periodical: pubg, pubg and print	5.6
Personal credit institutions	0.7
Personal services	7.0
Petroleum refining	1.1
Pharmaceutical priparations	5.6
Phone comm ex radiotelephone	1.9
Phono recrds, audio tape, disk	11.7
Photofinishing laboratories	3.4
Photographic equip and suppl	4.1
Plastic matl, synthetic resin	1.2
Plastics products, nec	2.7
Plastics, resins, elastomers	0.8
Poultry slaughter and process	2.5
Prepackages software	3.8
Printed circuit boards	1.2
Printing trades machy, equip	2.2
Prof and coml eq and supply-whsl	2.0
Pumps and pumping equipment	1.6
Radio broadcasting stations	5.2
Radio, TV Broadcast, comm eq	1.2
Radio, TV, cons electr stores	4.1
Radiotelephone communication	3.7
Real estate investment trust	1.9
Refrig and service ind machine	2.1
Retail stores	4.6
Rubber and plastics footwear	7.9
Sausage, oth prepared meat pd	9.6
Security brokers and dealers	1.8
Semiconductor, related device	2.0
Ship and boat bldg and repairing	0.5
Shoe stores	5.4
Skilled nursing care fac	1.7
Soap, detergent, toilet preps	9.9
Spec outpatient facility, nec	1.0
Special clean, polish prips	16.1
Special industry machinery	4.1
Sporting and athletic gds, nec	6.4
Srch, det, nav, giid, aero sys	4.3
Sugar and confectionery prods	12.7
Surgical, med instr, apparatus	1.2
Svc to motion picture prodtn	2.0
Tele and telegraph apparatus	0.7
Television broadcast station	3.2
Textile mill products	0.9
Tires and inner tubes	1.9
Unsupp plastics film and sheet	3.0
Variety stores	1.6
Video tape rental	2.0
Water transportation	7.3
Wmns, miss, chld, infnt undrgrmt	4.2
Women's clothing stores	2.6
Womens, misses, jrs outerwear	3.1
Wood hshld furn, ex upholsrd	2.5

Source: Advertising Ratios & Budgets. 18th ed. Published by Schonfeld & Associates, Inc. Reproduced by permission.

improvement—and to detours when necessary. It is a means of communicating your thoughts. It makes your reasoning visible. And understandable. But it is not an order from central headquarters to be followed blindly and without insight. Rather, it is a pledge of allegiance to the future of your business.

Summary

Whatever size your business is, you need a written marketing plan. Your plan is a good one if an outsider who doesn't know your business can understand it without anyone explaining it.

Before working up your plan, think about your marketing: who your target customers are, how you can relate to them, where you can appeal to small niches in the total market. Try to analyze which 20 percent of the market (or your customers) accounts for 80 percent of the sales. Decide on primary and secondary objectives.

Analyze your competition, too—their weaknesses, strengths, share of market, and share of voice. Figure out how you can position your store or product or service to make it distinctive, to make it stand out from the competition.

Try to understand the geographic, demographic, and psychographic aspects of your target customers: where they are; how they are identified by age, sex, income, family size, and their life-styles.

Organize your marketing plan to flow first through a situation analysis and a look at the problems you face and the opportunities they present. Then state goals and objectives, with an advertising plan or strategy to meet them—the "what we want to say and do" of the plan. Next comes a creative plan, or a "how we will say and do it" plan. The media plan follows, detailing when and where the advertising will appear. The following section pulls together the plan for integrated marketing communications—sales promotion, direct response, and public relations. Last, review the entire plan, write up a management summary, and move it to the head of the plan.

To set up a budget for advertising, work out a suitable ratio of advertising expenditures to sales, using ratios from your industry or from retailers as a guide. Or relate your advertising share of voice to your share of market, recognizing that share of market almost inevitably follows share of voice. A third method is to determine the cost of attaining your advertising objectives and then budget the needed amount.

Finally, think of your marketing plan as a road map that makes your reasoning clear and that shows where you are going and how you will get there. It is always subject to change and improvement.

PART TWO

WHERE DOES ADVERTISING COME FROM? HOW IS IT CREATED?

The problem with today's advertising is not so much its monotony and inanity. The problem with advertising is that most ads and commercials are not talking to people's needs and wants.

— Don E. Schultz and Stanley I. Tannenbaum,
Essentials of Advertising Strategy

CHAPTER FOUR

The Creative People Needed: Who Does What

KEY TERMS

answer print
art director
audio
bids
body copy
brag and boast copy
captions
casting
collateral use
color separations
competitive consumer benefit
comprehensive layout
computer animation
copy
copyrights
copywriter
creative strategy
creativity
crew
cutline
display copy
dye transfer
estimates
frames
gaffer
grip
headlines
jingles
kerning
key fact
keyline
kill fee
lead paragraph
license to use
line art
location
mechanical
mixing
perceptions
producer
progressive proofs
pub-set
reproduction proof
retouching
rough cut
scratchboards
script
the shoot
slice-of-life approach
slogans
sound effects
stock photographs
storyboard
subheads
tag lines
talking head
tape transfer
tone
typography
usage fee
Veloxes
video
work print

A prominent advertising man named Harry Jacobs has said that "creativity is the one and only thing" that advertisers "can't really do for themselves."

Creativity

Just what is **creativity?** It is easier to describe what it is not than to describe what it is. Creativity in advertising is not drama or entertainment. It is not innovation. It is not a shouting voice or powerful music or words printed so large that you have to hold your newspaper at arms' length to read them.

Creativity is the process that finds the most promising way for you to tell your prospective buyer about the benefits of your service or product or store. The more unique or innovative or dramatic or entertaining you can be in the process, the more creative your advertising will be. But the name of the game is to show the benefits. Nothing else matters.

One way or another, you or your staff can manage to handle most aspects of your advertising program, such as working out your marketing plan, figuring out what media to buy, developing the traffic patterns and time lines, following up on results, and making improvements. But in your small business, you have neither the time nor the skills to teach yourself or someone else the creative process that produces advertising. When it comes to conceptualizing and actually creating your advertising, you need people who already know how to write copy, design layouts, and direct performances. You need professionals. We will discuss shortly who they are and what they do. But first let's go back to a subject we covered in the preceding chapter: your creative strategy.

You Gotta Have a Creative Strategy

The heart of your company's advertising is its creative work: ideas and the ways in which it "executes" them. Ideas and execution together become what the advertising professionals call the **creative strategy.**

Your company doesn't have to be big or national or even regional to need a creative strategy. Retailers with one shop or a small chain, manufacturers with a single big-ticket product or a line of inexpensive small items—all use creative strategies to help their advertising programs work.

The Creative Strategy Development Form on page 46 was developed by two advertising professors, Don E. Schultz and Stanley I. Tannenbaum, of Northwestern University's Medill School of Journalism. Both have extensive experience not only in teaching but also in practicing the art of advertising.

When your creative people go to work on developing strategy, the first thing they will want to know is what is the **key fact** we are dealing with? You may think of it as the key problem. How many key facts do they want you to identify? Only one: The one fundamental to your marketing situation. Your key fact may be that you are introducing a new product. Or that your sales have leveled off. Or that you have added a feature or a service or improved something that your customers perceived as a drawback.

Looking at the key fact, your creative people will want to know what is the marketing problem that advertising can solve. If your key fact is that you are introducing a new product, the marketing problem may be how to bring your product to the attention of people who need it—even if they don't realize they need it. More than two generations ago, nobody knew they needed Scotch-brand cellophane tape. In 1950, nobody knew they needed Xerox copiers. And only a few years ago, nobody knew they needed 3M's Post-its. Advertising showed them they did.

If your key fact is that your sales have leveled off, your creative people might say that the marketing problem advertising can solve is to get people to use your product more. If you agree with them, say so—on paper. Put your key fact, along with a brief description of the problem that advertis-

CREATIVE STRATEGY DEVELOPMENT FORM

A. THE PROBLEM

1. The Key Fact
2. The Marketing Problem Advertising Can Solve

B. THE CREATIVE STRATEGY

1. What Is the Product? Or Service?
  a. In reality?
  b. As perceived?
2. Who Are the Prospects?
  a. Geographics
  b. Demographics
  c. Psychographics
  d. Media patterns
  e. Buying/use patterns
3. Who Is the Principal Competition?
4. What Is the Competitive Consumer Benefit?
5. What Is the Support for the Benefit? The Reason Why?
6. The Target Market Incentive Statement
7. What is the Tone of the Advertising?
8. What is the Communication Objective?
  a. What is the main point?
  b. What action should be taken?

Source: Schultz, Don E., and Stanley I. Tannenbaum. *Essentials of Advertising Strategy.* Lincolnwood, IL: NTC Business Books, 1988, 55. Reproduced by permission of the publisher.

ing can solve, on your office wall or conference room corkboard.

Now your creative people will zero in on your product. How does it work? What does it do—exactly? Where do its parts come from? By poking and prying and demanding answers to penetrating questions, your creative people might soon know more about your product or service or store than you do. They want to be loaded with facts, even those you consider inconsequential, about the product you are going to be selling.

But they won't stop with just the facts. Next, they'll want to know about **perceptions.** What do people *think* about your product, service, or store? How do they *feel* about it? Do they have warm feelings you can appeal to? Cold feelings you must overcome? And what do they think about the entire field of business you are in?

To come up with sound answers to questions like these, you and your staff must stop and think. You may be able to provide answers out of your experience. Or you may have to get some research done. Gathering information costs money and takes time, but it can be a valuable drill. The important thing is to help your creative people form an accurate picture of the product, service, or store you expect them to sell.

Your creative people will need yet another accurate picture, one of the person who is expected to buy. Whether this is a potential customer or a regular customer, the creative strategy must detail his or her geographic, demographic, and psychographic characteristics. In other words, you need to identify and specify the audience you want to reach. And don't forget that those prospects who are the same geographically or demographically may be quite different psychographically—and vice versa. In addition, you must help your creative people get a fix on your typical customer's reading, listening, and viewing habits (which media are the most influential? Which are the least?) and on his or her buying habits.

More questions. Your creative people will want to know about your competition. Who are your leading competitors? What do they offer that you don't, and what do they *seem* to be offering that you don't seem to be? What are their shares of market? How much are they budgeting for advertising?

With answers in place, you and your creative people are ready to pinpoint your **competitive consumer benefit.** This is the most important thing you can tell your customer about, because it is the "what's in it for you." And that is the only thing any prospective buyer wants to know. You may be selling a lawn mower that is economical to run, but simply saying so does not express a competitive benefit. "Costs less to run than mowers half as powerful" offers a worthwhile competitive benefit. Or you may be selling on price. "Get a mattress and box spring set for less than the department-store price of a mattress alone" states a competitive consumer benefit. So does "Finally, a powerful pain reliever that's not a pain to open," a headline that tells people who don't need childproof pill bottles that Tylenol has a competitive benefit for them.

In the examples above, notice that the advertiser is not simply giving the audience a descriptive feature of the product. To say the lawn mower is not a gas-guzzler or the mattress and spring set is low-priced or the Tylenol bottle is the plain old-fashioned kind would not give the audience—the target market—any helpful benefit.

Next, you and your creative people must think about how you back up the benefit. What is the "reason why" the reader, listener, or viewer should decide (subconsciously, in most cases) that the benefit is believable? The advertising copy for the lawn mower may describe a drivechain that gives the blades more cutting power and the wheels more pull than anything else on the market, while the carburetor barely sips gasoline. The mattress headline itself invokes the reputation for quality that department-store bedding is presumed to enjoy. The Tylenol headline offers the implicit idea that if you have arthritis or are just plain annoyed by childproof caps, you won't have to wince when you open this one. All are *sensible* reasons why.

With so much background and discussion now behind you, the next step urged by the Medill professors is something rather grandiose they call the Target Market Incentive Statement. Don't let it scare you. All they are asking you to do is put down on paper a single sentence that pulls your creative strategy together. "For homeowners, ours is the lawn mower that works harder at less cost."

"For anyone, ours is the mattress and box spring set that is department-store quality but that is priced lower than the department-store price for a mattress alone." "For older people, Tylenol is the pain reliever that is powerful and that comes in an easy-to-open bottle." In effect, your Target Market Incentive Statement is a comment on the obvious, but you will find it valuable to state it and keep it ready to refer to.

Then there's **tone,** next to last on the list compiled by Professors Schultz and Tannenbaum. Tone is not what you say, it is how you say it, how you look, and how you sound. It is typefaces and music and voice and scene and lighting. What is the tone of my advertising? is a question that you must address at the creative strategy stage of your planning. Do you want your tone to be strident, yelling and screaming in print or in broadcast? Do you want it to be quiet, dignified, and confident? Or light and playful if not downright comical? How serious is your message? How lighthearted? What is the tone that is most appropriate for your product, service, or store and that will set you apart from other advertisers—in particular, your competitors—and help make your message believable?

The final point in your creative strategy is yet another question: What do you want to have happen when your advertising appears? This question breaks down into two parts. Think them through with your creative people, then write down your answers. The first part is, what should the reader or viewer or listener "get" as the main point of your advertising? What idea or message or impression should come through? "I should buy Tylenol because I know it's powerful and now I know I won't have to struggle with some childproof cap." "I should go to that bedding store because it's foolish to pay department-store prices when I can get the same quality for so much less." "I should get that lawn mower because I'll save on gas and get the job done faster and better."

The second part of the question is, what do you want your audience to actually *do* as a result of your advertising? Again, it may seem obvious, but put it down on paper. You want the person who sees your advertising to take some specific action: You want them to buy the lawn mower, bedding, or Tylenol; tell someone else about it; think better of you and your product, service, or store; send for more information; call an 800 number...

All of the eight points on the Schultz-Tannenbaum form add up to your creative strategy. Think of it as the foundation upon which you and your creative people can build a forceful selling message.

Who are these creative people we've been talking about? They come in three groups: copywriters, art directors, and production people.

The Creative Type

Let's face it. Creative people are different. They have an extra gene that makes them excellent problem solvers and idea getters. One of the best textbooks written for college advertising courses describes the personal characteristics of creative people:

> Although everyone has some problem-solving abilities, certain traits seem to be typical of creative problem solvers. The first is that they soak up experiences

like sponges. They have a huge personal reservoir of material things they have read, watched, or listened to, places they have been and worked, and people they have known.

Research has found that creative people tend to be independent, self-assertive, self-sufficient, persistent, and self-disciplined, with a high tolerance for ambiguity. They are risk takers and they have powerful egos. In other words, they are *internally driven.* They don't care much about group standards and opinions. They are less conventional than noncreative people and have less interest in interpersonal relationships.

They have an inborn skepticism and very curious minds. They are alert, watchful, and observant. They reach conclusions through intuition rather than through logic. They also have a mental playfulness that allows them to make novel associations. They find inspiration in daydreams and fantasies, and they have a good sense of humor.

In general, creative people tend to perform difficult tasks in an effortless manner and are unhappy and depressed when they are not being creative. In addition to having many positive characteristics, they also have been described as abrasive, hard to deal with, and withdrawn.

What characteristics do creative thinkers *not* exhibit? They are not dogmatic (although they can be stubborn), and they have little patience with authoritarian people. They don't follow the crowd, and they like being alone. They aren't timid, and they don't care much what other people think.[1]

You would have to search hard to find a better description of the type of person who can create effective advertising for your small business. Such a person may be good with words or good with pictures or good at directing the performances of others. Once in a while, but only rarely, you will find someone who is good at both words and pictures, but chances are such a person is *good* but not *great.* Even more rarely will you find someone who is a triple hitter, who can do really good work in all three areas.

Creative people enjoy digging into a problem; wallowing in it; looking at it from the outside in and the inside out, upside down and backward. They revel in knowing everything there is to know about your product, service, or store. And they can't wait to tell others about it.

They are just as eager to find out everything they can about your customer or prospect. With their vivid imaginations, they can empathize easily with your prospect, knowing just how he or she thinks, feels, and reacts.

Then their creative natures cannot resist finding ways to bring the two—your product, service, or store and your customer or prospect—together. They will try to persuade the prospect or customer by appealing to his or her emotions—the feelings and senses that are excited by such things as fear, love, food, and humor.

You Gotta Have Words: The Copywriter

The writing that appears in advertising is called **copy.** The person who creates it is

1. Wells, William, John Burnett, and Sandra Moriarty. *ADVERTISING Principles and Practice, 2nd ed.* © 1992, pp. 390–391. Prentice Hall, Englewood Cliffs, NJ. Reproduced by permission of the publisher.

the **copywriter.** A good copywriter is adaptable, capable of writing in a variety of styles to fit the subject at hand. He or she is like a reporter, eager to dig in and get the facts, then tell them to the reader or listener. But the advertising copywriter lacks the cynicism of the news reporter. Rather, the copywriter has a certain enthusiasm that is contagious and that helps put zing into the copy. The copywriter can get excited about almost any interesting project and, as a result of his or her natural inquisitiveness, can learn the most technical details and find ways to communicate them clearly to others.

That curious mind looks for whatever is unique about your product, service, or store. The creative person wants to know how your product is formulated or manufactured and how it performs when the customer uses it. Or what step-by-step procedures occur as you provide your service. How about the past? What is the history of your small business, and what is unique about it? Is there something unique and intriguing in your packaging or product name? What message does your price convey: Inexpensive? Pricey but worth it? Highly expensive? Then there's the general category to which your product, service, or store belongs. If there is not too much that is unique about your own product, can the curious mind find something that is unique about the entire category, something that no one else has exploited, that you can claim as your own?

The search for the unique may take the copywriter into the plant where the product is made, to see firsthand how it is produced. He or she will want to take the product home (if possible) and use it, wear it, eat it, or cook with it. If you are a retail advertiser, he or she will want to spend time in your store regularly, observing how your customers react and make decisions, interviewing them, asking them what they like and don't like about your store and the items you are selling. If you are not a retailer, but your product is sold over the counter, the copywriter will stop in at various stores where your product is sold and make "store checks" on how it is displayed, how much shelf space it enjoys, and why people are buying or not buying it.

We should note, at this point, that these activities are not exclusive to the copywriter. The art director may be equally involved or may get into the act after the copywriter has done the preliminary work. Production people, however, come in later, as we shall see.

This deep probing and search for uniqueness is an attempt to find what advertising professionals call "the big idea." A big idea in advertising is one that stops the audience in its tracks. It is one that can change the opinion or attitude of the audience. It is one that plays directly into the advertising plan (the "what we must do" stage, remember) and the creative plan (the "how we will do it" stage).

An example of a big idea? Not long ago, Ford Motor Company realized they were manufacturing five of the bestselling cars and trucks in America. Their advertising plan ("what we must do") called for making Americans aware of this fact. Their creative people came up with the big idea: to pile these five cars and trucks on top of one another. Television viewers watched a popular spokeswoman, wearing hiking clothes and boots, climb to the top of the pile while telling the story—all in 15 seconds. This big idea came directly from the uniqueness of Ford's situation. It was a dramatic translation of a record-breaking sales success into an arresting visual that was simple, clear, and memorable.

Good copywriting calls for a style that fits the subject. In most cases, you want a natural-sounding, conversational style. The writing style sets the *tone* of the advertising, as mentioned earlier.

Good copy speaks directly to the reader, viewer, or listener. It says "you" frequently, extending a circle of intimacy to make "you" a part of the family of users of the product or service. If the copy starts saying "we," it becomes what is known as **brag and boast copy.** In advertising as in other walks of life, few people pay much attention to braggers and boasters, because these people don't answer the "what's in it for me" question. Yet if you pick up any newspaper, you will see ads with boastful headlines that say, for example, "We know pools" or "We go the extra mile" or "How do we describe our new home-equity loan? Special!" Such headlines offer the reader no benefits. They waste advertising dollars.

The heart of good advertising copy is simplicity. Sentences are short. They don't need formal structure. They come alive when you use action words. Visual words. Words that put sound into the ear. The great Russian novelist Dostoyevsky (who, so far as I know, never wrote ad copy) once said to a student, "No! No! The penny did not fall to the floor. The penny went hopping and clinking to the floor." A good copywriter sends pennies hopping and clinking to the floor, creating action before the reader's eyes and putting sound into the reader's ears.

Copywriters can usually work in any of the print or broadcast media. Some, however, have more of a knack for one medium or another, so in dealing with a copywriter you should be on the lookout for a specialist if you are concentrating on a single medium. And you should welcome a generalist if you are planning a broad-based program that will run in several media (see also Chapter 8 and Chapter 9).

Writing copy for each of the media calls for particular skills and techniques. Different media demand different vernacular. To discuss your advertising sensibly with your creative people, you should know what the key terms are and what they mean.

Print Copywriting Terms and Techniques

Advertising in the print media, mostly newspapers and magazines, communicates with its reader through two types of copy: **display copy** and **body copy.**

Display Copy

This is the big stuff. It is what your eye takes in at a glance when you skim through a publication. Three basic elements are considered display copy, but all three are not required, in fact, none of the three is required, to make an ad.

- **Headlines.** The headline is the grabber. It must immediately get the reader's attention by stating something provocative enough to make the reader want to stop and read the body copy. The headline should promise a benefit to the reader.

An effective headline is selective. It seeks readers who have an interest in the product or service being advertised. Like a heat-seeking missile, it zeroes in on its target audience, the audience you have described in your marketing plan.

The headline does another job. It answers the question that is likely to be uppermost in the reader's mind: What's this ad *about?* The headline reveals the subject—which specifically is your product, service, or store and which more generally is the category to which your product, service, or store belongs.

How important is the headline? According to researchers who have studied advertising readership, 80 percent of the people who read a headline do not read any more of the ad. They turn the page.

- **Subheads.** After a headline has grabbed the reader's attention, eye-catching and informative subheads can help pull the reader in. A subhead may appear just below the headline at the top of the ad. Or several subheads may appear throughout the body copy if the body copy is more than a paragraph or two in length. When a subhead appears at the top of the page, it is smaller in size than the headline; when subheads occur in the body copy, they are set in boldface and are slightly larger than the copy. Subheads work functionally to carry the reader along into the story your ad is telling. They lend emphasis. They call out to the reader, "Look! This is important. Better read this."
- **Captions.** These explain or interpret any illustrations found in the ad, such as photographs or artwork. The caption, also called a **cutline,** is the next most frequently read thing after the headline in any advertisement. No matter how obvious you think an illustration will be to the reader, you should never put one in an ad without a caption that explains it or reinforces some part of the ad's message.
- **Tag lines and slogans.** A tag line wraps up your message, usually at the bottom or end of your advertisement, with a memorable line or phrase. Usually it is a line featured in any ad you run: "A Shop for the Lady Who Expects the Best in Style and Service" or "Affordable Computer Solutions for Small Business & Home Users" or "You'll Never Get Rich Paying More for Less."

  What is a slogan? It is a tag line repeated so regularly and frequently that your readers recognize it, expect it, and would miss it if you left it out.

Body Copy

This is the text. If the headline pulls readers into the advertisement, the body copy has to keep them there. The first few words, or **lead paragraph,** are critical. They must be so intriguing that the reader, no matter how busy or distracted, cannot resist reading on.

Body copy delivers your complete sales message in as concise a form as possible. Here claims are made, proof is offered that validates the claims, and specific reasons are given why the customer should buy.

The style in which your body copy is written should match the subject. For a serious business-to-business ad, copy is direct and simple, even if the subject is complex. If technical terms must be used, make sure they are terms your readers understand. Don't use the jargon of your business or industry to try to make your ad look smart. Watch out for the pompous word or phrase. Readers who feel they are being talked down to are not likely to become customers.

Body copy for consumer products and services is written in many styles, from simple, descriptive narrative to dialogue between two or more people.

Your closing paragraph should ask for the order, just as a good salesperson would. Or it should make some call to action: "Send today" or "Stop by today" or "Call our toll-free 800 number now" or even a twist like "Go see all the others first."

Tip: If your ad is selling on price, watch the meaning of words. There is a difference between "savings," which is money you put into the bank to earn interest, and "a saving," which is what you get if the price is reduced. Don't insult the intelligence of readers (or listeners) who may know the difference and will wonder why you don't.

Radio Copy

The copywriter working in radio advertising writes for the ear. Probably no other medium is more challenging to write for, because the audience is listeners who are not listening. Rather, they are driving cars; jogging; doing their homework; hanging out with pals; washing and ironing; repairing cars; or getting breakfast for the kids, who are about to miss the school bus. They are doing everything *but* paying attention to the radio. And you want them to hear your message.

A well-rounded copywriter will be adept at getting the attention of a distracted audience. The copywriter knows what a personal medium radio is, how people relate to it as a steady friend who is always there in the background and how they create their own mental pictures to go with the words and sounds they hear.

The job of the radio copywriter, then, is to get and hold attention. How? By using unusual sounds, by creating a jingle, by having someone shout in a harsh and intrusive voice, by setting up a dramatic situation in which two or more people perform a miniature play, by using preposterous humor—the ways are endless.

The copywriter also realizes that the listener cannot "turn back" the advertisement to hear it again, the way a reader can flip back the page. Words and sentences must be simple and direct. Key phrases must be repeated. In fact, in radio, repetition is fundamental.

Some elements of radio copy you should know:

- **Sound effects.** A clever sound engineer in a recording studio can come up with any sound a copywriter calls for, either by finding it on records and tapes in an effects library or by creating the sound in the studio. Through sound effects, commercials can take the listener to a fire, to a howling gale, to the ocean, to a busy city street, or to a quiet cow pasture.
- **Jingles and music.** An old adage in advertising says, If you have nothing to say, sing it. That is not true. Time and again in radio and television, music and rhyme have proved highly effective in estab-

lishing and maintaining a product signature. A familiar jingle, once it has become established through repetition, cuts through the background and reaches the listener who is not really listening. If the jingle is light and lively and fun to hear, it is instantly recognized as a friend.

But a jingle works better as a reminder than as a conveyer of new information about your product or service.

Music has another important use in radio advertising. It creates and sustains a mood: lighthearted, somber, slow and easy, fast-paced. In a couple of seconds, a musical phrase can establish the feeling or emotion you want for your message. Playing "under," or as background, it can then maintain the mood throughout your commercial.

- **Time.** Advertising on radio is measured in seconds. You buy 10, 20, 30, or 60 seconds of airtime. That's all your copywriter has to work with. At between two and three words per second, your message must be skillfully tailored to attract attention, promise some benefit, urge the listener to do something, and give a credible reason for doing it, all the while making sure the listener knows that it is *your* product, service, or store that the advertisement is talking about.
- **Script.** A common format has long been established in radio copywriting. Everything that is spoken is typed double-spaced in upper- and lowercase on the right-hand two-thirds of the page. Everything that identifies who is speaking (ANNOUNCER, 1ST VOICE, 2ND VOICE, LITTLE GIRL'S VOICE) and everything that identifies other sounds (MUSIC, SFX [for SOUND EFFECTS]) is typed entirely in CAPITAL letters on the left-hand third of the page. This format makes it clear to all hands—the announcers, actors, and technicians—just what is to be done.

Television Copy

Nothing else in all of advertising can do what a television commercial can do. It can vividly demonstrate what a product is and does and how people react to it. Its essence is action. It puts sight and sound together, and each reinforces the other: You see what you are hearing about, and you hear about what you are seeing. The television commercial becomes a form of reality as strong as the reality that millions of viewers find in sitcoms, soap operas, and made-for-television movies.

There are many commercials that television viewers like. They get a kick out of them. They enjoy the brief but dramatic story lines, some heartrending, some downright funny, that are often more entertaining than the so-called entertainment they interrupt. But often viewers don't like to admit it. They resent the interruptions. They zap out the sound or briefly channel surf. They get up and go to the bathroom or the kitchen.

Your copywriter knows this. He or she knows that the task is to keep viewers in front of the television set, with their eyes on the tube and their ears open. It is not an easy task. Sight and sound must work together at all times. If they do not, the distraction is immediate and severe. Research has shown that viewers will remember your product and remember it more strongly (and, presumably, longer) if they hear its name as they see it. If you are demonstrating a key point, the words that viewers hear must be about that point. Whatever is seen must be heard and whatever is heard must be seen. This may seem obvious, but if you watch television commercials closely for an evening or two you will see plenty of advertising money being wasted on commercials that break the proven rules, that create confusion, and that insult your intelligence.

Television Terms and Techniques

The copywriter sets up a script for television that is similar to the radio script. The page is divided vertically, with **VIDEO** directions on the left and **AUDIO** on the right. Words that are to be heard on the sound track are double-spaced under the AUDIO heading. Under VIDEO the copywriter describes, in single-spaced CAPITAL letters, what is to be seen on the screen, including directions for camera movement. Directions for MUSIC and SOUND EFFECTS (SFX) are in CAPITAL letters at appropriate points on the AUDIO side.

Like a playwright, the television copywriter describes in the VIDEO directions the elements that the producer and director will need to know in order to bring the scene and action to life. This includes the setting—an interior such as a living room, store interior, kitchen, auto showroom, bathroom, dining room, or office or an exterior such as a backyard, downtown street, ballpark, swimming pool, or auto dealer's lot—and any props that are important in depicting the scene. Lighting is described, too, so that the producer and director know whether special equipment is needed to "create" things like brilliant sunshine, soft moonlight, or romantic candlelight. In brief, the copywriter's script must detail every element so that there is no guesswork. This is important, because you are paying by the minute for an expensive camera crew. Finally, the script calls for each specific title—one or more words that are seen on the screen—and provides a description of its size, its background (if any), and its length of time on the screen.

The television copywriter's script may call for one of dozens of conceptual approaches. For many years, one of the most popular was the **slice-of-life approach,** in which actors performing the roles of ordinary folks dramatized the point the commercial was making. The **talking head** approach features an individual, either an announcer or a well-known celebrity, speaking directly to the audience. The popularity of raucous, fast-paced MTV music videos has led to more and more commercials that offer only blink-of-the-eye glimpses of the actors, the scenes, and the product, creating an overall effect that can be exciting and memorable.

Some other terms and techniques you should be aware of:

- **Storyboard.** To help you and the producer and director to visualize the television commercial, the copywriter's script is often turned into a storyboard by an art director. Somewhat like a comic strip, the storyboard is a series of side-by-side drawings or **frames** that show in a sequence of stills the action expected in the commercial. Captions under each drawing state both the

VIDEO directions and the AUDIO (words) to be heard. How many drawings are needed? As many as it takes to visualize the action. Half a dozen frames are enough for some storyboards. Others need 15 or 20 frames. The length of the commercial is, of course, a factor in the length of the storyboard. The most common commercial lengths today are 15 seconds and 30 seconds.

- **Film.** For many years, the majority of television commercials were photographed on 35mm or 16mm film. After the film is shot, and after all editing work is done, a film-to-tape transfer is made so that the television station can transmit from videotape to the cable or broadcast audience.
- **Videotape.** With the great improvement in the quality of videotape in recent years, more and more commercials are made directly on videotape. Editing equipment has become highly sophisticated. The computer has made it possible to create ingenious special effects. And, unlike working with film, you waste no time waiting for processing.

Tip: With the latest software, you can now make storyboards right on a desktop computer, complete with sound and motion. Check out such software programs as Adobe Premier, Adobe Photoshop, Elastic Reality, and Macromedia Director.

Everybody Is a Copy Expert

This is a well-known saying in the advertising business. Someone has said that there are three things in the world that everyone thinks they can do better than anyone else: coach a football team, judge a beauty contest, and write advertising. Let the pros do all three.

You Gotta Have Design: The Art Director

How your store or product or service "looks" in advertising depends on your **art director.** He or she is trained to think graphically, with an eye for design in everything from newspaper ads to television commercials. Working closely with the copywriter, the art director first comes up with a visual concept or idea, then draws a rough layout of an ad for the print media or a rough storyboard for television. Next, through a series of meetings with the copywriter and with you, the advertiser, the layout or storyboard is refined and detailed (the layout becomes known as a "comp," or **comprehensive layout**). Finally, the art director works closely with all those involved in the actual production of the ad, preparing it for the printing press or for broadcast. Let's look at what the art director does in each of the major media.

Art and Photography for Print Advertising

Once the concept of the print ad has been determined, the art director must make a number of decisions. The first is whether to use photography or artwork. Fashions and furniture, as a look at most furniture retailers' or department-store ads will show you, look best in artwork drawn by skilled artists. Automobiles and food (especially in four-color ads in magazines) and most business-to-business subjects look best in realistic photography.

Each decision provokes another. If the print ad is to feature photography, who is to take the picture? Your art director is likely to have a Rolodex loaded with photographers, each of whom has a specialty of some sort: food, tabletop close-ups, location shoots, high-fashion cosmetics, factory interiors, you name it.

If the ad requires artwork, who will draw or paint it? Again, your art director knows who is best at loose, flowing watercolor washes; tight and realistic Norman Rockwell–type renderings of typical Americans; black-and-white pen-and-ink drawings (known as **line art**); **scratchboards;** pastels; or felt-tip pen work.

The point when using photographs or artwork is to fit the style of the illustration to the subject: to your store or product and to the tone. If you are a retailer, you know the consumer wants to see the merchandise. Your art director should play it up big, whether you are showing your products in artwork or photographs.

The layout your art director designs will tell the reader a lot about the kind of business you are running. An ad crammed with dozens of items each screaming its price says you are a discount store, drug store, or supermarket. An ad featuring one large illustration surrounded by generous white space, with an intriguing headline and short, well-spaced blocks of body copy, conveys an entirely different tone and image.

Tip: If you are a retailer, notice how many advertisers in your newspaper make the mistake of sticking their store names at the tops of their ads. No self-respecting art director would do this, but countless retailers, lacking professional art direction, let the salespeople from the media design their ads, with this unfortunate upside-down result. Readers, who start reading at the top of an ad, will immediately go on to something else if they find nothing more inviting than your store name at the top. The logical place for your name, along with address and phone number, is at the conclusion of your message.

You should be aware of a number of practical steps that your art director must go through before your print advertising is produced. Once you and the art director, usually along with the copywriter, have agreed on the conceptual layout and determined whether to use artwork or photography for the illustration, it is the art director's job to get **estimates** and **bids** on the job. He or she calls in those artists or photographers considered best qualified, shows them the layout, and discusses the specifications and logistics involved, including day of shooting and delivery date for finished work. The briefing should include the planned usage for the art or photograph (in which media, repeated how frequently). Three types of bid or estimate are commonly used:

- **Competitive bid.** All competitors are given the same layout and specifications, and the job is awarded to the lowest bidder.
- **Comparative bid.** All are given the same layout and specs, but when the bids come in, the talent of the bidder

and the quality of the work he or she produces is also considered. The low bidder does not necessarily get the assignment.

- **Single bid.** Here, only one bid or estimate is requested. Why? You may be dealing with an artist or photographer with whom you have worked previously and from whom you have gotten good-quality work at prices you know are fair. Or you may have selected the artist or photographer based on his or her unique style, talent, or skill (never forget that talent and skill are two different things: coming in on time and within budget is a *skill,* which is distinct from *talent*).

Understand the Copyright Law: Get Permission

The United States Copyright Law of 1976 says that **copyrights** of art and photography are owned by their creators. The work may not be reproduced in whole or in part without the permission of the creator. That means that if you want to own all reproduction rights to the material created for your use, your photographer or illustrator must sign an agreement transferring the copyright to you. According to the Copyright Law, such rights may be wholly or partially transferred or assigned, so you may name specific uses and accept assignment only for them. Some of the uses:

- **Publications.** This includes newspapers, Sunday supplements, trade and consumer magazines, in-house publications, and freestanding or bound-in inserts. You can sometimes save some money if you buy only a specific use, such as inserts, rather than the entire publications category—if you are sure that's all you need.
- **Point-of-sale.** Historically, this category was called **collateral use.** It includes signs, leaflets, brochures, countertop displays, direct-mail circulars, etc.
- **Out-of-home.** Counted here are posters that are not at point-of-sale, painted signs or "bulletins," 30-sheet posters, bus-shelter and transit ads.
- **Packaging.** Cartons, wraps, etc.
- **Television use.** Because of collective bargaining agreements in force between the broadcast talent unions and the networks and stations, any television use of your artwork or photography will probably have to be negotiated separately. Talk to the station where you are planning to buy commercial time.
- **License to use.** Sometimes you simply pay for a license to use a photograph or piece of artwork rather than for a full transfer of rights. When you "buy" stock photography, for example, you are not buying it, you are being licensed to use it.

Some businesses are satisfied to use their standard purchase orders as proof that an illustrator or photographer has assigned copyright to them. To avoid possible future problems, however, an assignment agreement is safer. See the box on 60 for a sample assignment agreement for artwork or photography.

If the photography or artwork for your ad calls for any person to appear as a model who can be identified, either your art director or the photographer should have each such person sign a Model Agreement (see sample agreement, 61).

SAMPLE ORIGINAL PHOTOGRAPHY OR ILLUSTRATION ASSIGNMENT

For valuable consideration, receipt of which is hereby acknowledged, I hereby assign to (Name of Advertiser) (the "Company") all of my right, title, and interest in and to the original photography or illustration described below (the "Material"), including, without limitation, the copyright therein, and/or the right to register the copyright therein, and any and all renewals and extensions of any such copyright, in the United States and every other country in the world. I further agree to execute any documents necessary to effectuate the foregoing.

I warrant that I am the sole owner of the Material and the copyright thereto, that it is my original work, that it has never been published, that I have no contractual or other arrangements that would interfere with or prevent this assignment and transfer of all my right, title, and interest in the Material and that it does not infringe the privacy or other rights of any person.

I also agree to indemnify and hold harmless the Company and its respective directors, officers, agents, employees and assigns, and anyone authorized by any of them, from and against any and all claims, liabilities, losses and damages, including reasonable attorneys' fees, caused by or arising wholly or in part out of the reproduction and/or publication and/or any other use of the Material and to defend at my expense any litigation instituted by others against any of them resulting therefrom.

Advertiser: ______________________________

Photographer/Illustrator: ______________________________

Address: ______________________________

____

Social Security or
Tax Identification No.: ______________________________

Description of Material: ______________________________

Date and Place Work Done: ______________________________

Consideration: $__________, payable ______________________________

Signature______________________________ Date ______________

Name______________________________

Source: American Association of Advertising Agencies. *Guide to Buying Advertising Art & Photography.* Copyright 1991. Reproduced by permission.

SAMPLE MODEL AGREEMENT

TO:

Date ____________________
Job No. ____________________
Product/service ____________________

RETURN TWO SIGNED COPIES OF CONTRACT WITH INVOICE IN TRIPLICATE TO:

(Company Name) ____________________
(Address) ____________________
(Phone) ____________________

Please indicate job no. on all invoices & correspondence.	

DESCRIPTION

You, ____________________ , agree to furnish your services as model, to appear and pose in photographic session(s) on date(s) and location(s) specified below for ______(company name)______ (hereinafter "we" or "us").

Date(s) and time(s) ____________________
Location(s) ____________________
Media ____________________
Use period(s) ____________________
Territory ____________________
Compensation ____________________

Your signature and ours shall constitute this a binding agreement between us.
I certify that I am 18 years of age or older and have every legal right to enter into this agreement.

ACCEPTED AND AGREED TO: ______(Company Name)______

Signature ____________________ By ____________________

If signer is under 18 years of age, parent or guardian must sign below.

I, as parent/legal guardian of ____________________,

do hereby consent to all of the foregoing and execute this document in evidence thereof.

Signature ____________________

Source: American Association of Advertising Agencies. *Guide to Buying Advertising Art & Photography.* Copyright 1991. Reproduced by permission.

What if your art director has to cancel a photo shoot or the rendering of artwork after it has been ordered? You will probably have to pay a **kill fee,** depending on how far the planning and work have progressed. If models have been booked, expect to pay them, too. Good idea: Make sure your art director discusses such contingencies at the time when he or she is first negotiating the assignment.

The Television Art Director

Like the top-notch copywriter, the professional television art director brings a rich background of interests, experience, skills, and talent to the job. He or she can conceptualize scenes and action and will draw rough storyboards to show what is to happen on film or videotape, refining these in close cooperation with the copywriter and with you, the advertiser. The television art director has a strong sense of style—of how the setting for the commercial must be "dressed" with props and scenery—and of dramatic action and timing. The "look" of your advertising, from when you first see a storyboard until you watch your commercial on your television set at home, is the responsibility of your television art director.

In fact, the television art director is a combination of artist, cameraman or photographer, set designer, costumer, and director. He or she is a storyteller capable of touching the hearts of the audience to make them cry or tickling their funnybones to make them laugh.

More specifically, the television art director knows the techniques of television: how superimposed titles work to emphasize key copy points, when to "cut" to a tight close-up of your product and how long to keep it on-screen, why a conceptual approach that you like may be too costly to produce and how it can be adapted to the restrictions of your budget.

A particularly useful skill for television art directors to have today is **computer animation**. It is fast replacing the costly and labor-intensive methods of traditional animation, which involved drawing one frame at a time, photographing each, and running them at 12 to 16 frames per second to create motion.

Somebody's Got to Pull It All Together: The Producer

Once you have approved of the words and design worked out by your copywriter and art director, someone has to make it all happen–on time and within budget. That someone is the **producer.**

An advertising producer is like a theater or Hollywood producer: He or she creates and supervises the atmosphere in which creative and technical people work together to achieve results. The producer must be a needler, a worrier, a detail person who leaves no loose ends. The producer must *produce.*

Print Production

If your advertising department consists of one copywriter and one art director, each of whom may be freelancers, you should expect all phases of production to be handled by your art director. In a larger department that is producing a steady flow of ads, you may have a production specialist who keeps track of traffic flow and due dates; lines up estimates and bids; dispenses purchase orders; and sees that every step, from comprehensive layout through final proofs and shipment to the media, is completed correctly, as well as on time and within budget.

Several key steps occur in the process of getting photographs or illustrations ready for print advertising.

Preproduction

After bids are reviewed, the job is awarded to the photographer or illustrator. Before a purchase order is issued, final negotiations should review any changes in the specifications, noting how contingencies such as cost overruns or changes in the planned use of the material will be handled. No work should begin before the purchase order is signed by the photographer or illustrator. Specific dates should be set for seeing proofs, contact sheets, or preliminary sketches, as well as finished prints or art—and enough time should be allowed for any revisions.

A preproduction meeting should bring together the people responsible for each aspect of the photo shoot: the photographer, art director, copywriter, food stylist, props stylist, casting director, wardrobe stylist, location scout. *Note:* Some photographers charge separately for "prep days," while others include preproduction time in their total fees. Avoid unwelcome surprises by asking your photographer about his or her policy.

Products and Props

The production person should request any samples of your products or packages required for the shoot well in advance, so that the photographer can determine whether any changes need to be made. Often, packages and labels have to be color corrected or models have to be constructed.

Casting

If your shoot calls for models, your producer or art director may round up composite sheets (several photos of a model printed on a single 8½-inch-by-11-inch sheet) or models' sample books for review, either directly or through the photographer. After you or your advertising director approve of the model selected, the model is booked and issued a purchase order and model release. Make sure the release is signed before the shoot begins.

Props and Wardrobe

It is usually cheaper to rent the props and wardrobe needed for a shoot than to buy them. Prop and wardrobe stylists, often freelancers hired by the photographer, are experts at locating items that are appropriate for the mood or image you are trying to create. If any items must be purchased, they belong to you after the photo shoot. Whether they are rented or bought, all items should be listed on an inventory sheet and copies should be given to the stylist, the photographer, and the art director or production head. When the items are returned, they should be signed for.

Retouching

In getting photography ready for reproduction, any of three types of retouching may be used.

- **Electronic retouching.** Original color transparencies (slides) are converted to a digital format. From this, as part of the color separation process, retouched separations, transparencies, or color prints are made.
- **Original or duplicate transparencies.** Studio photography of tabletop still lifes is often done on large format 8-inch-by-10-inch color film, large enough to retouch fairly easily. Studio work involving people usually calls for faster shutter speeds and greater depth of field, using 35mm or 2¼-inch-by-2¼-inch film. To retouch these photos, the original is enlarged to 8-inch-by-10-inch size as a duplicate transparency.
- **Dye transfers.** Sometimes considerable retouching is needed. A **dye transfer** is made from the original color transparency, and enlarged color separations enable a retoucher to make almost any necessary change. However, some fidelity or sharpness may be lost in making the enlarged dye transfer separation.

Stock Photographs

Often photographs exist that are suitable for use in your advertising. Your art director will know of stock houses that maintain extensive libraries of photographs, both black-and-white and color transparencies. Some stock houses keep inventories in a wide variety of categories. Others specialize, concentrating on such subjects as agriculture, sports, industry, pets, children, antique autos, to name just a few.

Photos in stock libraries are usually the work of professional photographers. Quality varies, however, both in technique and in subject matter. Look closely for anything in a stock photo that may make your advertising seem out of date—a man wearing a wide-collared shirt and a wide necktie, a street filled with cars that were new 10 to 15 years ago, a lady with a Minnie Pearl hairdo. Some stock photos have been in some stock houses for a long time. (That is not necessarily a fault, however, for often an art director is looking for a photo from an earlier period.)

Here's how buying stock photos works. Your art director contacts the stock house and asks to see slides or prints of a certain subject. The stock house is likely to charge a research fee for pulling suitable material from its files and delivering it. If you later use one or more of the photos, the research fee is dropped or is credited against the use fee. *Important:* Make sure careful records are kept on how many photos are ordered for review, how many arrive, how many are sent back. If *original* slides are ordered and received for review, take special care. Stock houses are likely to charge outrageous fees for damaged or lost slides.

When a photo is selected, your art director contacts the stock house to discuss the **usage fee.** The fee will be based on the total circulation anticipated for your advertisement (that is, how many times it will appear in how many publications, each with how many readers), as well as the length of time over which it will appear. You may want to negotiate exclusive usage during your period of use, so you effectively retire the photo from the stock house's library for that time. You don't want to see "your" photo in someone else's ad.

Tip: If the stock photo you want to use shows any people who can be identified, make sure the stock house has signed releases from them permitting the use of their likenesses for advertising purposes. Don't run the risk of a claim for damages for unauthorized use.

Typography, Keylines, Progressive Proofs

While the photography or illustration is being produced, your art director or production person orders **typography**—the headline, subheads, and body copy set in type. Most type today is set by computer, with literally thousands of typefaces available and with ample opportunity for **kerning**—the movement of individual letters and spaces to shape headlines and enhance the attractiveness of the layout of words in your ad. A skillful art director or type director understands which faces are most suitable for the character of your product or store and for the particular message your ad is sending to the reader. Specifying type is, in fact, an art.

Using **reproduction proofs** of the type (that is, proofs of suitable quality for use in printing), your print producer or art director next prepares a **mechanical,** also known as a **keyline,** on which every element of your advertisement is positioned. Either a film or photoprint is made from the keyline to be sent to the publication in which your ad will appear.

How does your production person know what specifications to follow in preparing your ad for a publication? He or she consults the industry bible, *Print Media Production Data,* a quarterly published by Standard Rate & Data Service that lists production requirements for newspapers and magazines nationwide.

Some publications want positive prints (known as **Veloxes**) and some want negatives. If you are running a color ad, the publication wants the separate negatives for red, yellow, blue, and black (called **color separations**), as well as **progressive proofs** that show all four colors singly and in combination.

Pub-set Ads

Many periodicals are ready to help you with production. Newspapers in particular offer **pub-set** services. This means that the publication sets the type for your ad—and actually does more than that, helping with illustrations and with basic design or art direction. The trouble with such services is that often the quality is not very good. Ask your newspaper salesperson to go through a recent issue, marking off all the pub-set ads. Notice how many contain a jumble of various typefaces and sizes, as if the typographer wanted to show off how many different type fonts were at his or her disposal. Such ads subject the reader to an uninviting mishmash of type. Note, too, the number of pub-set ads that (as mentioned earlier) simply put the name of the advertiser at the top of the ad, failing to give the reader any promise of a benefit. Check out pub-set offers carefully.

In 1990, an unusual kind of production help was offered by the *Syracuse Herald-Journal* of Syracuse, New York. The paper provided several major advertisers with equipment—including Macintosh computers, software, printers, and accessories—and training, so the advertisers could design and create their own ads. A local department store, a department-store chain, a large furniture retailer, an electronics company, a large grocery-store chain, and a real-estate firm all joined Syracuse Newspapers, the Herald-Journal's parent company, in what the publication called partnerships. The partnerships were limited to advertisers who placed a high volume of ads and who had staff that could handle the work. Some continued to ask the newspaper's advertising staff for help, while others simply turned in computer disks with ads ready for reproduction.

The cost to the newspaper was about $20,000 per partner, but the return was far greater. The advertisers in the partnership signed multiyear contracts, producing 10 to 15 percent more advertising than previously.

Producing Your Television Commercials

Television production changes constantly. New technology is always being created that requires the development of new skills. Because of this, you must think of television production not as a body of rules and habits but as an evolving creative process. Production experts offer two basic pieces of advice:

- **Treat every project as an original.** Start over every time you make another commercial.
- **Never assume anything.** Constantly check and recheck to make sure that what you want and expect to happen is, in fact, happening.

To get your television commercial made, you have two choices: to produce it yourself or to have the production handled by the television station on which the commercial will appear.

Producing it yourself means you put someone else in charge as the television producer—your art director, your advertising director, or a freelancer. Your producer then hires a production company. Such companies are located not only in the major production centers—New York, Chicago, and Los Angeles—but also in many cities across the country.

Start production by getting bids from at least three production houses. They should use a bid form provided by the Association of Independent Commercial Producers (AICP), which is universally accepted, to give you either of two types of bids:

- **Firm bid.** The production company agrees to do the job for a fixed price. You agree not to change the specifications. If the company gets the job done for less than the quoted price, it keeps the difference. If the company exceeds the budget, it takes the loss.
- **Cost plus fixed fee.** Here, the company estimates the cost and adds a markup or fee. No matter how much the job costs, the fee stands, and you pay the total cost. If the job costs less than estimated, you gain the saving.

The production company's bid is not the total cost you must anticipate. Unless the production company is to handle each of the following, your television producer will need to get an estimate or bid on the costs of film editing; music and sound effects; talent, such as actors, announcers, extras, musicians, singers; and any special effects such as animation.

Television production has three phases: preproduction, production, and postproduction.

Preproduction

In one or more meetings, all hands involved—the copywriter, art director, film or videotape director, casting director, set designer, location scout, the stylists (for props, costumes or wardrobe, setting, food, hair and makeup, etc.), and advertising director—go over the script or storyboard in detail, planning exactly what footage or tape is to be shot and how it is to be done.

Tip: An experienced and knowledgeable director, by carefully going over your commercial scene by scene and moment by moment in a preproduction meeting, can suggest ways not only to reduce costs but to save time during the shoot, when time is most expensive. A skilled director more than earns his or her pay. Nothing is more valuable than getting full agreement, at the preproduction stage, on all aspects of the commercial to be shot.

Production

This is the shooting, or **the shoot**. Among the elements you should know about are the following:

- **Location or set.** Usually it costs less to scout a location—interior or exterior—than to build a studio set. However, if special lighting control is needed, a set may be more practical. Props are rented as needed.
- **Nights, weekends, and per diems.** Production crews expect to be paid a premium for night shoots. Weekends and holidays mean double time. Location shoots out of town mean per diem expenses for meals and lodging.
- **Talent.** The performers' unions (Screen Actors Guild, New York Extra Players, Screen Extras Guild, American Federation of Television and Radio Artists, and American Federation of Musicians) enjoy strong contracts that may affect your commercial, depending on which stations you are buying in your media plan. So you may or may not have to use union actors or announcers. Check with the salesperson who is selling you the time.
- **Crew.** Most shoots call for a crew that includes most of the following: director, assistant director, cinematographer or video-camera operator and assistant, script clerk, properties manager, **gaffer** (electrician), **grip** (general helper), sound recorder, sound mixer, boom operator (if a hanging microphone is used), makeup person and hair stylist, and video engineer or operator (if shooting videotape rather than film).

Postproduction

Now all the production elements come together to make your commercial ready for broadcast.

- **Editing.** The director, producer, art director, and copywriter review all the film or tape shot during production and decide which "takes" or single shots are the best to edit together. A **rough cut** is assembled, which shows the sequence of shots but does not include the optical effects or finished sound track. Next comes a **work print,** followed by the **answer print** or final form.

  You or your advertising director must take the responsibility for seeing and approving each of the editing steps. If you wait until the last step, then see something you want changed, you will have to pay heavily for the privilege of going back to an earlier step.
- **Mixing.** This step follows the rough cut, but it is so important you should think of it as a secondary editing phase. All elements of the sound track—music, voice-over, lip-synced dialogue (the voices of the performers seen on camera), and sound effects—are carefully combined or "mixed" to match the picture.
- **Tape transfer.** At the answer-print stage, the picture (if it is on film) and track are transferred to videotape, color corrections are made, opticals (visual effects such as fades, dissolves, zooms) and titles are finalized. Your commercial is ready for use by broadcast or cable stations.

Other Considerations

How long does it all take? Allow at least 10 weeks from the time you approve the storyboard to the completion of your commercial. Expect to spend 4 weeks getting estimates and bids and awarding the job to the production house, then 6 weeks getting the commercial ready for use.

Suppose the television station on which you are buying time offers to produce your commercial. Chances are it can complete the job in less time than a production company can and at less cost. Whether the quality of production will be comparable depends, of course, on what kind of work the station is used to doing and what kind of production house you might hire to work for you. To resolve the question, ask the station to screen its sample reel for you and ask two or three production houses to screen theirs. Look and listen carefully, critically, and more than once. Often, if you run a reel again immediately after screening it, you notice things you didn't catch the first time—a wrong inflection on a word, an ungrammatical sentence, a sequence of action that is silly or annoying, audio that doesn't agree with the video.

Remember, viewers are going to see your commercial over and over. Any distraction that prevents them from seeing and hearing your message will do you no good. And if you are questioning an apparent fault, don't be silenced by producers or salespeople who say, "Nobody will know the difference." There is always someone who knows the difference. You will never lose a customer who doesn't know the difference, but why risk losing one who does?

Producing Your Radio Commercials

Much of what you have just read about producing your television commercials can be applied to radio commercials. Once you have approved the script, think in terms of preproduction, production, and postproduction. Someone must function as the producer, bringing together the talents of actors, announcers, musicians, and sound-effects specialists, while working against the pressures of time and budget.

Your radio producer should get bids or estimates from at least three studios or production houses. The production steps are a simplified version of those found in television: recording voices, music, and sound effects; then mixing them on audiotape to make a master from which duplicates can be dubbed to send to radio stations.

As in television, the station where you are buying time may provide production facilities and direction. Or it may provide copywriting talent to create "live" commercials that are read on the air by the staff announcer who is on duty when your commercial is scheduled. The cost of writing or production may be absorbed by the station if you are buying a heavy enough schedule to justify it, or you may be charged for the service.

What Makes Creative Work Good or Bad?

Two of the best authorities you can find, Northwestern's advertising professors Don Schultz and Stanley Tannenbaum, have summed up the virtues and the sins that make advertising interesting or dull. A list of these is on page 70, and it's worth mounting on your conference room wall.

Summary

Creativity is the process through which you find the most promising way to tell your customer or prospect about the benefit you are offering. A creative strategy will help guide that process, determining a key fact or problem that your advertising must address. By studying your product, store, or service; its competitors; and its present and potential customers; your creative people will determine the competitive consumer benefit you should be advertising.

The copywriter creates the words that sell your product, identifying its unique aspects and developing a memorable idea that grabs the attention of your audience. To understand advertising copy, you need to know the terms and techniques used in the basic media—print and broadcast—so that you know what works best... and why.

The art director creates the look of your advertising. He or she designs the layout and supervises photography or illustration for print ads and draws the storyboards for television commercials. The art director performs other important tasks as he or she follows the project through the production steps to its completion.

Print, television, or radio advertising are produced in three stages: preproduction, production, and postproduction. At each stage, specific steps should be followed and certain techniques should be used to get successful results that are cost-effective.

THE SEVEN HEAVENLY VIRTUES

First: Deliver a significant, competitive promise or benefit. It must, must come out of the product.
Second: Build a personality bank. In this bank are stored perceptions of your product or service. Every communication should make a deposit in the personality bank, building a long-term personality that is always welcome in the customer's home or office.
Third: Be specific. Pin things down, present evidence—facts—and the customer will reward you.
Fourth: Master the art of omission. The customer is interested in only one thing: simplicity—What's in it for me?
Fifth: Be direct. Make your point quickly and unequivocally. To be obscure or oversubtle is suicide.
Sixth: Know your customers. Make sure the ad talks to these customers in their language and depicts them the way they really are.
Seventh: Insist on the unusual, the uncommon, the unexpected. Never create trite, cliché-ridden advertising just because that's what everybody else is doing.

THE SEVEN DEADLY SINS

First: Advertising the advertiser. Running messages the advertiser wants to hear rather than messages the customer wants to hear—bombastic messages like, "We stand for quality!" or "We're proud of our record!"
Second: Making exaggerated, unbelievable claims. It is almost a rule: The less information and the less salesmanship in the ad, the more numerous and inflated its adjectives.
Third: The "one foot plus teeth" syndrome: people always standing within one foot of each other and always smiling. They don't talk, act, or look like real people.
Fourth: Art for Art's Sake and Copy for Tom's Sake. Art is the art director, and Tom is the copywriter. The sin is the attempt to create ads or commercials with elaborate pictures or drawings and tons of high-blown rhetoric. Everything in an ad should be functional. Nothing should call attention to the mechanics of the ad.
Fifth: Following the leader. Somebody gets a great idea for an ad. Then somebody copies them. And then somebody else copies them. Imitation is the sincerest form of boredom.
Sixth: Intimidation, or The Hard-Sell Fallacy. Battering down the customer's resistance—torturing him so much he'll say uncle and buy your product. Pile-driver layouts with mammoth type. Or shouting announcers on television and radio repeating so-called hard-selling lines ad nauseam. Remember, the hardest selling of all is gentle persuasion.
Seventh: Arrogance. Assuming that the customer will believe anything, proposing the preposterous, exaggerating the truth, overwriting in an attempt to overwhelm. It has been proven, time and again, that advertising is accepted by individuals only if it agrees with their experience or common sense.

Source: Adapted from *Essentials of Advertising Strategy* by Don E. Schultz and Stanley I. Tannenbaum. Lincolnwood, IL: NTC Business Books, 1988, 85–91. By permission of the publishers.

CHAPTER FIVE

Who Says It Might Work? Who Says It Did Work? The Role of Research

KEY TERMS

aided recall
animatic
attitudes
awareness
benchmark
bingo cards
buried offer
communications effects
diagnostic research
dummy advertising
focus group
image
market simulation test
posttesting
pretesting
qualitative research
readership test
recognition test
sales effects
split run
test market
theater test
unaided recall

Research in advertising and marketing is simply the study of human behavior. It examines *what* the consumer does and *why* he or she does it. *What* involves statistics. *Why* involves psychology. The key to understanding either is *method* in a scientific sense: Someone else, using the same step-by-step method you used, is certain to arrive at the same results.

Some people in business—especially small business—say they have neither the time nor the money to bother with research on their advertising. Why should you bother? Because, as Charlie Brower, whose career in advertising took him to the chairmanship of the giant ad agency BBDO, said, "No one should knock research who has ever been helped by a road map."

Research can help you, or whoever is creating your advertising, to understand your product or service and its market and to think like your prospect thinks and to feel like your prospect feels. Research gets you the facts you need. In many cases, it proves what you already suspected. In others, it disproves what you had assumed to be true. Does this mean you must lay out big money for primary research—information you collect from original sources? No. Leave that to the industry giants, like Procter and Gamble or Xerox or Pepsico. You can find secondary research—information that others have compiled and published—in the trade papers and magazines that serve your line of business and in the meetings and seminars offered by your trade or industry association.

However, there is sure to be some research pertinent to your particular marketing and advertising activities that you probably can afford and that will be valuable in planning and carrying out your advertising program.

Research on your market and prospects, as discussed in Chapter 3, gives you valuable help in setting the guidelines for your advertising strategy and the messages that carry it out. Your creative people have two subjects on their minds: *before* and *after*. What can they find out about awareness of your product, service, or store and attitude toward it *before* your advertising program begins? And what can they find out about it *afterward?* Overall, what can you and they determine about what might work in advertising and about what is or is not working now?

Setting Up Your Benchmark

In getting your program under way, you want to set some objectives. These should be directly related to the advertising strategy and creative strategy set forth in your marketing plan. Your objectives may be hard: to see how many inquiries the mail brings, how many 800 phone calls ring in, how many coupons come back, how many **bingo cards** (reply cards bound into trade journals with code numbers keyed to advertisements) ask for information about your product. Or your objectives may be soft: to increase **awareness** of or change **attitudes** toward your store or product or service. Your ultimate objective, of course, is sales—but keep in mind that unless advertising is literally your only sales effort, it is hard to prove that advertising is the sole reason for sales. Rather, advertising may change your **image** in the prospective customer's mind or may bring your name forward in his or her memory.

Research looks at your advertising in two different ways. One way tries to analyze the **communications effects** your advertising may produce. The other tries to measure its **sales effects.** Overall, your advertising objectives probably divide into three types: (1) teaching your prospect the facts about whatever you are selling to create, first, awareness of it and, second, understanding of it; (2) generating in your prospect some feeling toward what you are selling—an attitude toward it and a set of beliefs about it; and (3) causing your prospect to do something—to make an inquiry about your product or to buy it.

Think of the first two—teaching the facts and generating a feeling about your product or service—as communications oriented. Think of the third—causing action—as sales oriented. Test each *before* and *after* your advertising appears. What you find out before becomes the **benchmark** against which you judge what you find out afterward.

Pretesting Your Advertising

You can use a number of different methods to pretest the communications effects and sales effects of your advertising. No one method is right or wrong; each can contribute valuable information.

Communications Effects

Among the methods used to test the communications effects of your advertising are these:

Focus group. A small group of people (usually not more than a dozen) meets with an interviewer who shows them your advertising. The advertising may be in the conceptual or rough layout stage or in the more finished comprehensive layout stage. Storyboards of commercials may be shown by using slides or an inexpensive process called **animatic**—a word that comes from the patented Animatic, a filmstrip projector used by ad agencies in the early 1950s to show proposed commercials to clients. Several different creative approaches may be reviewed. The design of the ads and the points made in the body copy may be discussed. In fact, free and open discussion is encouraged. The professionals refer to this as **diagnostic research** or **qualitative research.**

Usually your copywriter and other advertising staff watch and listen to the focus group from behind one-way mirrors. Or they listen to audiotapes afterward. By listening to the focus group, they find out how effectively headlines communicate a consumer benefit, how convincing copy points are, why a reader would like to try the product or service or learn more about it, or why he or she couldn't care less about it.

How useful the focus-group interview is depends heavily on the skills of the interviewer. He or she must be careful not to let one or two aggressive or extremely articulate members dominate the group. All present must be encouraged to express their opinions and feelings frankly and without fear of ridicule by others.

Dummy advertising. Your advertisement, in comp layout, is placed in a typical position in a dummy magazine that contains other advertisements, as well as editorial features. Individuals are asked to read the entire issue and are then interviewed not only about the advertisements but also about the editorial matter. The researchers evaluate the readership of each ad, how much was recalled, and whether the opinions formed were favorable or unfavorable.

Theater test. For many years, television commercials have been tested in theaters before specially selected audiences. More recently, truck-sized mobile theaters large enough to hold groups of people have appeared at shopping malls, where the researchers recruit shoppers according to age, sex, family income, and use of products. The audience is shown commercials or print advertising and interviewed on recall, understanding, feelings, and whether they liked or disliked what they saw. Verbatim answers are later analyzed to determine whether the advertising communicated the intended message or any message that was *not* intended, as well as how those who saw it reacted to its elements—the look or sound of its words, the pictures, performers, and setting—and the overall tone.

On the air. Some research services are set up in certain test cities so that researchers can place test commercials within regular television programs. Viewers are phoned the day after your test commercial is shown. They are asked—in what researchers call **unaided recall**—if they remember seeing a commercial in your product category. If they do not remember seeing one, they are asked—in **aided recall**—if they remember seeing your commercial. The interviewer also asks the viewers if they remember specific copy points of the commercial.

Advertisers like on-the-air tests because the people who are interviewed see the commercials in their own homes, rather than in an artificial setting such as a mobile or fixed theater. But some say that recall of a commercial does not equate to understanding the message.

Testing commercials is considerably more expensive than testing print ads. As noted in Chapter 3, if the cost of research is greater than 5 percent of expected sales, it's not worth it.

Sales Effects

What about pretesting that promotes action and is sales oriented? Two types of tests are common.

Inquiry. This is a very direct way to check an ad's ability to generate sales. You run two or more versions of the ad, with variations in headline or copy but with the same offer of a free gift or a product sample "buried" (not displayed prominently) in the ad; this is know as a **buried offer.** The ads may run in sequence in separate issues of the same publication, or for a premium charge, you can arrange a **split run,** in which two versions of the ad are printed in alternating copies of the same issue as they come off the press. You can then count the number of replies to each ad to know which pulled best.

To test ads even more quickly, you can use a toll-free 800 number. Count the number of telephone inquiries received within 24 or 48 hours after your ad appears.

Warning: Every inquiry is not necessarily genuine. You may get people who simply want the product sample or the free gift but who will never become customers.

Tip: Don't try to test more than one element at a time. If you are testing two headlines, keep the body copy the same. If you are testing copy, keep the headlines the same. To test illustrations, keep headline and body copy the same. Otherwise, you will never figure out what is working or not working in your ad.

Market. If you are selling in more than one geographic area, you can think of one of the areas as your **test market,** where you run separate and distinctive advertising. Newspapers and broadcast are the most likely media for a test-market endeavor. Your objective may be either to see which advertising approach produces the greatest sales, or to see what is the optimum amount to spend on advertising to generate the optimum amount of sales.

An alternative to this method is market simulation testing. If you are selling consumer packaged goods, you may want to try a **market simulation test.** Respondents are shown a number of advertisements, including yours, before they go into a special store set up by the research organization. The "customers" are given seed money and invited to shop. Some days or weeks later, they are called and asked how they liked the products they "purchased," whether they intend to repurchase, etc.

Be careful not to get blindsided by pretesting. One major national company kept developing and testing creative executions of ads and commercials for a new dog food. Ultimately the company realized that the more the advertising made the food look appetizing to humans, the more likely they were to buy it for their dogs.

Posttesting Your Advertising

After your advertising has appeared, a posttest measures change. You want to know whether your advertising message has changed attitudes toward your company, product, or service; whether the advertising has affected the prospect's intention to buy; or whether the advertising has actually produced sales. Posttesting, like pretesting, can check out both the communications effectiveness and the sales effectiveness of your message. One of the most revealing studies on the effects of advertising was reported in 1993 by the International Mass Retail Association (IMRA), which conducted the study in conjunction with the Gallup research organization. The study, "Print Advertising and Its Impact on Consumer Shopping Behavior," reported that more than 80 percent of 1,000 consumers surveyed recalled reading an advertising circular for discount department and specialized mass retail stores, compared with 75 percent who remembered seeing a commercial on television, 53 percent who recalled reading an ad in the body of a newspaper, and 45 percent who remembered hearing a radio commercial. Furthermore, the study revealed that 78 percent of respondents who held onto the circulars used them to plan their shopping trips, and 47 percent took the circulars with them to the store. Sixty-two percent of respondents used circulars to make buying decisions at least once a month or more often. Readership was high, with 21 percent carefully reading all the circulars they received, and 38 percent glancing through them. The study clearly showed that, for mass retailers, advertising circulars have the strongest impact on shoppers.

Described below are the most common types of posttesting used to learn the effects of communications.

Readership Tests

You want to know if your ads are being recognized and read. A **readership test,** also known as a **recognition test,** checks on readership in magazines and newspapers. Usually a number of readers of the publication are interviewed, either in their homes or offices. They are asked if they have read the specific issue. If they have, they are shown ads—including yours—as they appeared in the issue, and the readers are questioned about each element in each ad: the headline, each block of copy, illustrations, and the signature or logotype. For each element, three scores are registered:

- *Noted.* This is the percentage of all readers of the issue who remember seeing your ad in the publication.
- *Associated.* The percentage of readers who remember seeing some part of the ad that identified your name or brand.
- *Read most.* The survey shows the percentage who read half or more than half of your ad.

Among the research companies using this basic technique, the best known is Starch INRA Hooper. Usually its test is partly paid for by the magazine being tested, as the magazine wants to find out about readership in order to support its sales pitch to advertisers. This helps keep down the cost to advertisers.

How dependable is such a test? Starch uses a strict screening system to make sure those it surveys are genuine readers of the issue of the publication that it is studying. And, in going through the issue, it uses extremely careful interviewing techniques to be certain respondents are identifying ads they really have seen and read.

Recall Tests

This is another test that depends on memory but, unlike the readership or recognition test just described, it is an *unaided* recall test. Those interviewed are asked at the outset to provide details of at least one editorial feature or article from the issue being studied. If they pass this step, they are shown cards listing products advertised in the issue and are asked to note ads they have seen. For each ad, questions are asked about what the ad said or showed and how well it persuaded the reader. The final score combines proved recognition of the advertiser's name, communication of the advertising idea, and the extent of a favorable attitude toward the advertiser or product or service.

The recall test helps you to find out how well your readers understood the idea of your advertisement. This depends on memory, so in a sense the test's accuracy and effectiveness depends on the memorability of the ads you are running.

Posttesting for the sales effectiveness of your advertising can be as simple as monitoring sales figures and relating them as best you can to advertising. You can do only that—relating sales figures as best you can—because so many variables other than advertising go into your total sales effort. Probably the only area in which advertising is an isolated selling effort is pure direct marketing (see Chapter 10). Among the helpful guides for this area of advertising research is the well-known Nielsen Retail Index, which monitors retail sales, inventory, share of market, prices, displays, and promotional work.

Some Research Things to Think About

Keep reading your trade publications and checking with your marketing consultants, creative people, and trade or industrial associations for the latest news about research, because improvements in research capability come fast with technological change.

For example: No sooner had the checkout scanner arrived in the supermarket than research outfits like BehaviorScan appeared. BehaviorScan invites single households to use encoded identification cards at the checkout. The store's scanner records, in the single-source data system, every purchase made by the cardholder. Test commercials can be cut into the cable television seen in the households within the system. Thus, the researchers can monitor nearly all supermarket purchases made by those in the system and can evaluate the effectiveness of the advertising the cardholders see. As more and more retailers of every kind install scanners and as we move closer to a cashless society, evaluating the effectiveness of advertising becomes more and more practical and reliable.

If you are a retailer, one of the most useful research tools you can use is the focus group. Use a trained research service. You should be able to learn a great deal about prospects' awareness of and attitudes toward your store—in other words, your image. You can also use the focus group to check out how easily understood—and how persuasive—a planned advertisement is.

Another way to test your advertising copy is to make up a direct-mail piece for a specific item you want to move, then send this piece to a limited number of customers. If it pulls well, you can feel confident about using the same copy and illustration in your newspaper advertising.

Tip: Wish you had an inexpensive way to research prospects? Sponsor a contest or sweepstakes. On the entry form, ask for name, address, age, and income (set up brackets by $10,000 levels so you're not seen as being too nosy) and include any other information you seek, such as frequency of visiting your type of store.

If you are a business-to-business advertiser and want to set up diagnostic or qualitative research—for example, focus groups—remember that the very customers you want to reach are probably busy executives who just don't have the time or inclination to sit down and chat in an interview session. Work with your research group to find a way to make the meeting attractive. Perhaps you could host a "working breakfast" or "working luncheon," with a guest speaker talking about a related subject; the focus-group interview then becomes an ancillary event—ancillary to the guests, but primary to you. The important thing about focus groups is to make sure the members are as representative as possible of the people you are directing your advertising to.

One more thing. Keep your perspective. Remember that the research setting is not the setting in which your advertising will normally be seen. People in the research setting, inevitably, are oriented to the task at hand. They know they are being interviewed. They may try to make comments or give answers that they think are expected of them. The skilled interviewer is alert to such things and tries to work around them. But the fact always remains that when your advertising appears in its natural setting, the atmosphere is different. And the reader's or viewer's response may be different, too.

If you are ready to conduct pretesting and posttesting of your advertising, or other market research, where do you find the specialists who do this kind of work? Contact your trade or industry associations. Ask the people who sell time and space to you at the media you are now using. Look in the Yellow Pages under *Marketing Research & Analysis* and *Marketing Consultants.* Then call in several likely research services and ask them to make presentations on how they work; whom they do work for; how extensive their experience is; what in-house facilities they have, such as conference rooms designed for holding *and observing* focus-group interviews; how quickly they report test results; and how much they charge for typical services. You may ask for competitive bids.

Summary

Research in advertising and marketing is the study of human behavior, involving statistics, psychology, and scientific method. Research can help you and your creative people understand your product or service, as well as understand how your customer thinks and feels about it. By studying awareness of and attitude toward your product both before and after your advertising appears, research can help you determine what might work and what is or is not working.

Research objectives should stem from the advertising and creative strategies stated in your marketing plan (Chapter 3). These objectives include analyzing both the communications effects and the sales effects of your advertising.

Pretesting may be done in several ways. Focus groups provide free and open diagnostic discussion of your planned ads or commercials. Dummy advertising tests place your ad in a realistic publication setting. Theater tests expose your commercials to the reactions of ordinary folks in shopping malls. On-the-air schedules in test cities test next-day recall.

Sales effects can be tested by soliciting inquiries through buried offers and split runs, as well as by using test markets or market simulations.

Posttesting measures changes in awareness, attitude, or intention to buy and changes in actual sales. One important study has revealed that, for mass retailers, the advertising circular has the strongest impact on shoppers. Readership or recognition tests dig into whether magazine ads are noticed at all, identified with your name or brand, or at least half read. Recall tests provide a score that reflects recognition of your name, communication of your advertising idea, and attitude toward your product, service, or store.

It is important to remember that, except in isolated cases such as pure direct marketing, sales result from many variables and advertising is just one of these. Bear in mind, too, that research is an ever-changing discipline, with rapidly evolving technology constantly bringing new developments.

If you are eager to conduct advertising research, or other market research, check out several research services carefully, doing your own comparison shopping and getting competitive bids.

CHAPTER SIX

Maybe You Should Hire An Ad Agency

KEY TERMS

account executive	*billing*	*marketing plan*
agency-client relationship	*commission*	*media buyers*
agency presentation	*compensation agreement*	*media planners*
art directors	*copywriters*	*spec work*

Advertising agencies are service organizations that developed not long after the Civil War, when publications gave their agents a commission (usually 15 percent) for selling advertising space. Gradually, the agents began to advise their clients on the preparation of the advertising as well. They also became independent business organizations, acting as agents for all the available media and becoming experts on their comparative values. For the past century, advertising agencies have created the advertising materials for their clients, the advertisers.

There are now about 12,000 agencies in the United States. They range in size from one-person shops to international giants employing thousands. Agencies are found not only in New York, Chicago, and Los Angeles, but in countless small cities and large towns. No matter where you are, you can probably find advertising agencies listed in your Yellow Pages.

Today's agencies are experts in all aspects of advertising and marketing. An agency's greatest value, however, lies in its expertise in two areas: creative work (that is, the creation and preparation of advertising) and media knowledge and skills (that is, the most efficient and effective placement of advertising). To get these skills working for your business is the main reason you hire an advertising agency.

As you begin to think about an agency, it is important not to think of it as just another supplier. Rather, the agency comes to you offering no inventory other than the talents and experience of its people. It knows that it can succeed as a business only if it helps your business succeed. If you establish an **agency-client relationship,** one of the greatest contributions you can make to your own success is to think of your advertising agency as your business partner.

What Does an Agency Do That You Can't Do Yourself?

An agency can do several things that are hard for you to do. One is to give you unbiased and objective counsel. Getting a fresh, outside viewpoint from someone who is not afraid to ask penetrating questions can be invaluable to you.

With that come two kinds of experience gained by working with other advertisers: First, the agency may have experience in lines of business similar to yours. Many agencies specialize. Apparel, automotive products, computer hardware and software, financial services, travel and resorts, food, household appliances—the number of areas in which an agency may have experience is endless. Second, the agency is sure to have experience in unrelated lines in the general field you are in—such as business-to-business, retail, medical-pharmaceutical, recruitment. Both kinds of experience are valuable, for they bring you professionalism.

Here is how that professionalism goes to work for you.

Knowing All About Your Business

An agency that is thoroughly professional sets out to know just as much as you yourself know about the product or service you are selling. How the product is manufactured or how the service is performed; how it compares to its competition; how it is packaged, priced, and distributed—*everything* about its advantages and disadvantages is grist for the agency's mill.

The agency looks just as closely at the market for your product or service. It wants to know not only who buys it, but who *might* buy it—among wholesalers, retailers, and consumers—and why. And when. And where.

It studies the ways you move your product or service to the market—your distribution system—and how your sales force operates. Can the agency know too much about the product or service you are selling? Never. That is one of the reasons why you must think of your relationship with your agency as a partnership.

Developing the Marketing Plan

The agency works closely with you to formulate your **marketing plan** (see Chapter 3). The plan puts down on paper every aspect of the marketing of your product or service, from when you first conceived of it to when the consumer makes the purchase. Covered in the plan are targets and budgets for package design, sales research and training, design of point-of-purchase displays and sales literature, publicity and promotion and advertising to the trade—not to mention advertising to the consumer.

Creative Work

Upon your approval, the agency goes to work to execute the plan. In developing the creative work, it first figures out what you should say about your product or service—the idea you want to get across—before determining *how* you can best say it. The agency works to find a concept that will separate you from your competition. A small-parts manufacturer, for example, may want to tell prospective customers that it makes absolutely reliable parts for use in complex machinery that must be absolutely reliable.

The execution of the concept is the "*how* you say it." If you are a small-parts maker like the Heli-Coil Company of Danbury, Connecticut, you are pleased when your agency comes up with the line, "We have a part in everything that flies—except a bird." That positions you as a hefty player in the aircraft industry and tells your audience in a memorable way that they can count on you. (Is that line, incidentally, an example of brag-and-boast copy? Yes, but it also offers a benefit: absolute reliability, a benefit much sought after by makers of machines on which lives depend.)

Agency creative people—**copywriters** and **art directors**—are experts at figuring out "how to say it" convincingly and memorably in whatever medium is best for reaching your target audience. They know that readers and viewers and listeners are constantly bombarded with advertising messages and that they grow more cynical and indifferent toward advertising every day. Creative people work skillfully to get the audience's attention and lodge a message, an impression, a perception about you in the minds of your prospects.

Production

Your agency handles the endless details of producing your advertising—making mechanicals and negatives for printing, audiotape and videotape and film for broadcast; checking on typesetting and computer graphics; casting models, actors, and announcers—checking back regularly with you for approval. The agency makes the recommendations. You make the decisions, for it is your money that is being spent.

Media

Hiring an agency also means that you don't have to learn all about the vast world of media (see Chapters 8 and 9). The number of choices about where to place your advertising message today is staggering. Agency **media planners** and **media buyers** understand broadcast, cable, print, direct response, and out-of-home media. Responding to your marketing plan, media planners weigh reach, frequency, continuity, and cost-per-thousand to give you what cliché lovers call the biggest bang for the buck. It's their job to deliver you the right audience.

It's the job of the agency media buyer to deliver that audience within your advertising budget. The buyer on your account goes to work to get the best deals possible. Often, using knowledge, experience, and sales skills, the media buyer can negotiate prices below those stated by a station's or publication's rate card. The buyer sets up the schedule—how many ads to appear in what positions in which publications, how many spots to be seen or heard at what times on which stations, and so on. The agency then signs contracts with the media.

Traffic, Distribution, Follow-through

Next, the agency has to make sure the right materials get to the right media at the right time to be printed or broadcast. Such distribution is a key service, relieving you of yet another logistical nightmare.

But it's not over then. Your agency follows through after the advertising has appeared. It checks on tear sheets, or clippings, from newspapers and magazines. It gathers affidavits from stations testifying that commercials were broadcast as scheduled. If it finds discrepancies from original orders, it demands adjustments and make-goods.

Finally, the agency bills you for space, time, and production costs. If you pay promptly, it passes along any cash discounts it gets from the media or others for on-time payment.

Prompt payment, by the way, is at the heart of the agency-client relationship. Your agency is not your banker. It cannot advance payments to media or production houses if it is not being paid by you.

Once your agency has developed an advertising campaign that zeroes in on your marketing objectives and target audience, and once the creative work has been produced and the media planners and buyers have sent it on its way, the agency does not sit back and relax. It immediately moves on to what's next?—evaluating, revising, checking on broadcast audiences and newspaper and magazine readership, making sure your advertising money continues to be spent as wisely as possible.

How Is the Agency Paid?

For many decades, big agencies serving national clients were happy to get the traditional 15 percent of the cost of media. That has changed. Today most big agencies find that they must work under any of several compensation arrangements.

Smaller agencies have long known this. They cannot operate successfully on the income from media commissions alone, for 15 percent of the cost of advertising in a trade or technical journal or on local radio cannot begin to meet an agency's payroll or overhead.

Compensation Agreement

The agency will want to get a good grasp of how much time and effort will be needed to service your account and will then negotiate a compensation agreement with you. It will probably be one of the following types:

- **Commission and fee.** If you are buying a minimum amount of time and space on a regular schedule, the agency accepts the 15 percent media **commission** and bills you for materials and services purchased on your behalf. In addition, it either (1) sets an overall additional fee, (2) determines a profit floor and a profit ceiling to which you make a commitment, or (3) establishes a minimum fee against which it credits the media commissions.

- **Fixed fee.** You agree to an overall fee in advance. It is then up to the agency to handle your business, meet its costs, and make its profit all within that fee. No media commissions come to the agency, as you pay the media directly.
- **Cost plus.** Here, the cost of handling your business is calculated after the work is done, based on hours put in by agency staffers.

If you are spending regularly in paid media, the first of these compensation arrangements is probably the best. But if your program is mostly in direct response, sales promotion, or public relations—each of which has no media commissions—one of the other two arrangements is more appropriate.

How Do You Find the Agency That Is Right for You?

One way to start is by looking at other peoples' advertising. Collect ads you admire. Make notes of radio and television commercials in your city, town, or market area that you find memorable and hard-selling—hard-selling meaning ones that convince you, not that yell and scream at you. Call those advertisers. Ask them who handles their advertising. See whom they recommend.

Depending on the size of your business, you may want to set up an Agency Selection Committee. It could include your president or CEO, your sales or marketing director (or both), your treasurer or chief financial officer, and any department heads who should participate in advertising/marketing decisions. Keep the group small—not more than half a dozen, at most.

Join your local or area ad club (see Chapter 13). It probably meets at least once a month for lunch or dinner. Schmooze. Meet people who sell time and space for the media. They know which agencies are good. Invite the good ones in to talk. Take your time—you're making an important decision.

At the reference desk of your library, ask to see *The Standard Directory of Advertising Agencies,* known as the "Agency Red Book." It lists more than 3,500 agencies around the country and includes headquarters and branch offices, memberships in associations, names of officers and current clients. The Red Book is updated every quarter, so it's an excellent guide.

Its companion is *The Standard Directory of Advertisers,* or the "Advertiser Red Book." Here you'll find 25,000 entries. If you want to know which agency created some advertising that you particularly like, this book will tell you. The book lists each advertiser's address, size, industry classification, officers, divisions, and which agencies handle which particular products or services. The book is updated annually.

Then there are the trade publications. *Advertising Age* and *Adweek* not only provide weekly news of the business but publish valuable special editions: *Advertising Age's* "Top 100 Agencies" and *Adweek's* "Agency Report Card" include many agencies that are glad to handle small-business accounts. (See also Chapter 13.)

Consider the A.A.A.A. Members

Look in the Yellow Pages under "Advertising Agencies." Note especially the listings gathered under the heading "American Association of Advertising Agencies—Members." A.A.A.A. members are the top-notch agencies. To belong to the association, an agency must have been in business for at least two years. It must pass a rigorous examination of its balance sheet by agency accounting experts at A.A.A.A. headquarters. The agency must be entirely independent—not owned or controlled by any advertiser, advertising medium, or supplier. And it must be elected by other members in its geographic and market area. Of every three agencies that apply for membership, only one is approved. Of the 12,000 agencies in America, only about 700 are A.A.A.A. members.

The size of the agency is not a factor in election. More than 60 percent of the members annually "bill" less than $10 million each. (*Billing* is a term for how much the agency's clients are spending in advertising.) Many A.A.A.A. agencies employ only a few people, but you can expect them to be the cream of the crop.

How does an agency's membership in the A.A.A.A. help you, its client? Membership in the association gives the agency access to a wide range of proprietary and confidential financial studies that help it to run its business effectively, giving you an agency operation that you can have confidence in. Membership also means that the agency can take advantage of the association's information service, a leading business library of extensive secondary research files on thousands of products, industries, and markets, plus more than 350 databases.

If you are a business-to-business advertiser who is trying to move into international sales, the A.A.A.A. can help your agency set up affiliations with agencies overseas and provide practical information on media and trade practices.

Finally, the smaller A.A.A.A. agencies have long been familiar with the concept of integrated marketing communications. These agencies have been producing not only paid media advertising but also comprehensive programs of direct response advertising, sales promotion materials, and public relations for many years. More than one such agency has had the experience of not only producing advertising but designing the front entrance, parking-lot gates, and the signs on the delivery trucks of retail clients—so all elements work together to create a positive impression on the customer.

The A.A.A.A. will be glad to send you its roster of members if you write to them:

American Association of
Advertising Agencies
666 Third Avenue
New York, NY 10017

Narrow Your Search

When you're getting serious about hiring an agency, put together a questionnaire to be completed by any you call or who call on you. Make sure the questionnaire asks about their **billing** (the dollar total that their clients spend on advertising or other marketing services), the number of

AGENCY QUESTIONNAIRE

1. What have been the agency's annual billings for the last five years?
2. If the agency has more than one office, what were its total billings last year?
3. What percentage of agency billings growth is from new business and what percentage is from existing business?
4. What is the range of advertising budgets handled? Also, what are mean and median budget levels?
5. How many nonclerical personnel does the agency employ?
6. What has been the agency's turnover rate among account executives over the past five years?
7. What is the agency's current client list?
8. Which clients were won in the past year? Which were lost?
9. What has been the agency's growth rate over the last five years in number of clients? How many have been lost in the last five years?
10. What services does the agency perform in-house? What services are subcontracted?
11. What experience does the agency have with our line of business?
12. How much of the agency's experience is with retail markets? How much with business-to-business markets?
13. Briefly describe the agency's most recent retail and business-to-business campaigns.
14. What have been the agency's three most effective campaigns? Why are they considered most effective?
15. What methods of compensation does the agency use? Commission? Commission-and-fee? Fixed fee? Cost plus?
16. Who are the individuals who will be assigned to the account as account executives? Creatives? Media? Others? What are the backgrounds of each?

Source: Maddry, Norwood. *"Selecting An Ad Agency—A 'Short Course'."* Bank Marketing, June 1990, 33-34. Reproduced by permission of Bank Marketing.

offices and their locations, an up-to-date list of clients, the names of all officers and department heads, the numbers of employees in various departments (for example, creative, media, account management, accounting/bookkeeping), accounts won and lost during the past two or three years, and capabilities in the integrated marketing communications areas of direct response, sales promotion, and public relations.

Send your questionnaire to the agencies that interest you—but not to everyone. Keep your list short enough to handle. Six to eight, at most, should be enough.

As you start looking for the right agency, be sure to consider any that have already worked for others in your general field—retail apparel, computer hardware or software, travel, restaurants, automobiles, banks, or whatever. These agencies will have sound experience that can be applied to your business. But be aware that a reputable agency will not take on your business if it already handles a direct competitor of yours.

Most agencies work hard at getting business. They keep prospect lists up-to-date. They make cold calls. Probably you have had more than one such call. Whether you first called the agency or it called you, the officers will want to meet with you to put on the **agency presentation**. This introduces you to the agency's people and their experience and abilities, the clients and the work the agency has done for them, and the success stories—all in greater detail than was provided on your initial questionnaire.

The agency will want to ask many questions so that it can come back on another day and make a detailed proposal on how it would handle your business. But don't expect the agency to develop creative work on a speculative basis. That would be unfair to it and to you, for the agency cannot yet know enough about your business to make productive advertising. Nor can it afford to put in the kind of time and thought that you can expect when you are paying for it. An exception is major national agencies, which often do **spec work** when soliciting the accounts of multi-million-dollar advertisers. You have probably read about this in the advertising columns. An agency can spend several hundreds of thousands of dollars this way, in man-hours and production costs. Sometimes it pays off. Sometimes it doesn't. And sometimes the prospective client pays big money for the spec work.

When the agency people meet with you again, encourage them to be frank in discussing how they see your business. Do you feel that they have a grasp of your markets and customers and competition? How does their strategic thinking grab you? Would you feel confident in having them as business partners?

If you are getting serious about a particular agency, call their clients. *And* call their *former* clients. Find out what makes the current clients happy *and* what made the former clients leave.

Don't be surprised to learn that the size of your budget influences the agency's interest in you. The agency officers who meet with you will be frank in telling you whether they consider your business worthwhile to their business.

The Right Chemistry Counts, Too

Frankness is important. You and the agency people must "hit it off" if the relationship is to be successful. Probably few business relationships are as dependent on the chemistry of personality as the advertising agency-client relationship is.

The right chemistry is especially important in the direct working relationship between you or your advertising manager and the agency person you will see the most of: your **account executive.** The account executive is to the agency's work what a theater or movie producer is to the play or film. He or she is a planner, an expediter, a finder of ways and means, a person who must create a work atmosphere in which a host of talented people and technicians coordinate their efforts to produce the finished product—on schedule and within budget. The account executive represents the agency when in your office and represents you—the client—when at the agency. And always, the account executive keeps the customer in mind, pushing for advertising or other integrated marketing communication that gets through to your target audience.

Knowing all this, you will want to be certain that the agency you are considering tells you—early on—exactly who will be handling your account...who will be *your* account executive. Watch out for senior people who make the agency presentation when soliciting your business, but whom you may not see much of later on. You want to know whom you are going to "live with" after you award your business to the agency.

When you and the agency agree that you should march down the aisle together, you will be asked to sign a written agreement. Among the handful of points the agreement should make are these:

- The agency will not take as a client any direct competitor of yours—unless you say it's OK.
- The agency will secure your approval in advance on all advertising expenditures.
- The agency will pass along to you all cash discounts—if you earn them by paying promptly.
- You will not engage any other agency to handle any part of your advertising for the same product or service unless the agency says it's OK.
- You will pay the agency before the agency has to pay the media.
- If you should decide to terminate the relationship, you will continue to pay for work that appears during a termination period—usually at least 90 days. This allows time to complete work that is in the pipeline or to fulfill contracts already made for advertising space or time.

Final note: Once you have appointed an agency, let the officers who called on you from other agencies know why they did not land your business. You'll be helping them do a better job in their next presentations. You'll establish goodwill for your company and yourself. And who knows? The day could come when you might want to talk with one of the agencies again.

Summary

An advertising agency is a service organization. You can find one or more in most cities and large towns. An agency's greatest value to you is its ability to produce the creative work—writing and design—for your advertising and to plan and buy the most effective advertising media for reaching your target audience. One of the most important contributions you can make to a successful relationship with your agency is to think of the agency as your business partner.

Your agency offers professional skills in analyzing every aspect of the product or service you are selling, from manufacturing through distribution. It formulates your marketing plan, determines *what* you should say about your product or service and, even more important, *how* you should say it. It plans the media through which you can reach your target audience most efficiently and effectively and buys space in publications or time on the air or on cable at the best price possible.

The agency is paid in any of several ways: media commission and fee, fixed fee, or cost plus. Prompt payment by you is crucial to the success of the relationship, for no agency can function as your banker.

You can find the right agency for your business by carefully examining other companies' advertising and by finding out who handles the advertising that you find intriguing or that you know is successful. You can also look in the Yellow Pages or talk to the agencies that make cold calls on you. You will find it worthwhile to consider seriously those agencies that are members of the American Association of Advertising Agencies (A.A.A.A.), for their reputations are well established and well deserved.

When you find an agency that seems right for you, and if the chemistry between its people and yours seems positive, you should sign a written agreement to do business together.

CHAPTER SEVEN

Or Should You Get Freelance Help?

KEY TERMS

employee leasing	*moonlighter*	*percentage deal*
independent contractors	*out-of-pocket costs*	*retainer fee*
letter-of-agreement	*per-assignment fee*	*work-made-for-hire*

If you decide that you don't want to set up your own in-house advertising department, and if you decide that you don't want to invite an advertising agency to handle your ad program, your third choice is to put freelancers to work.

In your particular business, there may be peaks and valleys in the advertising work load—seasonal times, such as Christmas, spring planting, back-to-school, when you must plan and execute a heavy schedule of ads and commercials. It would be impractical to maintain an advertising staff year-round, so you decide to use freelancers. Actually, you could make a fourth choice, keeping a very small staff on hand to cover your needs during slow times, then hiring freelancers to help out during peak times.

There are probably very few businesses in which you can find as many freelancers as advertising. If you decide to buy creative work—copy, art, and production—à la carte, you have plenty of choices. So it is important to look carefully at the background of anyone you hire. Check references. Carefully examine samples of the writer's or artist's work. Ask penetrating questions about how a design was arrived at or why copy is slanted a certain way. More than one copywriter or art director has been known to carry someone else's work around to interviews. The person who did the work will have answers. Someone who did not do the work may try bluffing his or her way through.

Who Are the Freelancers?

Creative people who freelance come in four types:

- *Moonlighters.* One of your best bets for getting good creative work is to hire copy and art people who are working for advertising agencies. They know the business. Their creative brains are up and running and in high gear. Why do they freelance in their spare time? They want—or need—more money than they are making at their salaried jobs. Or, like many advertising people, they are compulsive writers or artists who want additional challenges. Your main risk in hiring a **moonlighter** is that he or she may suddenly become too busy on the regular job, so be prepared for that possibility. If you are producing enough advertising to warrant maintaining a small stable of writers and artists—maybe two or three of each—who know your business, you protect yourself against a phone call that says, "Geez, I'm sorry, but I just can't get to you this week—we're in a big push at the office."
- *Retirees.* Advertising is a young people's business. So advertising people voluntarily retire young or succumb to attractive early-retirement offers, often well ahead of the Social Security years. If they are talented, creative people, they will quickly find themselves up to their ears in boredom, and they will welcome freelance assignments. Your risk? You want to be sure that the retiree is in tune with today's advertising and is not living in the past. Some copywriters and art directors are old and out of ideas at the age of 40, while others are young and full of creativity at 55 or 60 or even older. Check samples carefully to be certain that work being done today does not look or read like work that was done 10, 20, or more years back. You want contemporary design and typography. You want copy that is lean and mean. Make sure your retiree talks today's language in both words and pictures.
- *Between engagements.* Advertising is a volatile business. Agency people change jobs often, sometimes because they move to better-paying jobs at other agencies, and sometimes because they get laid off when clients take their business elsewhere or cut their budgets. Talented people who may be out of work through no fault of their own welcome freelance assignments. The risk you run is that they may get new jobs sooner than they expected and suddenly they are too busy to work for you. If you are getting good talent in the meantime, however, that is a risk worth taking.
- *Full-time freelancers.* Some people have no intention of commuting into a city and working in a typical office atmosphere. They thrive in the independent home studio or home office. And with today's computers, modems, fax machines, and overnight delivery services, they can serve clients anywhere. In particular, two-income families with young children find success freelancing

their art or writing skills. Many parents who have built up sound backgrounds in advertising are freelancing around the schedules of preschool or elementary-school children.

While we are looking mainly at freelance creative talent, you should be aware that advertisers of all sizes, all across the United States, have made various à la carte services well established and accepted. You can find freelance help for any step in the development of your advertising, from initial strategic marketing planning to product positioning, from television and radio production to managing your entire advertising program.

Advertisers who work with such independent resources often say they get better results than they do with an advertising staff—better talent, faster response, greater objectivity, and more direct communication. Many find that costs are lower, too. Such results are not guaranteed, however. You must select your freelancers carefully, taking the time and trouble necessary to investigate their credentials and make some well-informed judgments.

In addition, when you work with freelancers, you or another member of your staff must be ready to handle the planning, management, and coordination of the various parts of your advertising program. That someone may even be yet another freelancer who has advertising management skills.

When you are considering freelance talent, what characteristics should you look for? In addition to talent and experience in advertising, look for a high level of self-discipline and plenty of self-confidence. And try to find evidence of empathy—the ability to identify with you and your company, product, service, or store and to understand what you are all about.

Where Do You Find 'Em?

To find freelancers who can do the job for you, talk with people whose judgment you can trust—other advertisers; the media people who sell space and time; and the printers who get out the best-looking brochures, catalogs, annual reports, direct-mail circulars, and newspaper inserts. They know who is talented, who delivers on time, whose work is clean and contemporary and least in need of revision. For tips on where to meet and schmooze with advertising people, most of whom will be glad to share information about freelancers, see Chapter 13.

Look also in the Yellow Pages under such headings as "Advertising Agencies & Counselors," "Advertising—Direct Mail," "Art Studios, Artists—Commercial," "Marketing Consultants," "Product Design & Development," "Sales Promotion," and "Writers." In addition, many employment agencies listed in the Yellow Pages can provide temporary marketing personnel.

You may also want to send for the guide *Directory of Independent Advertising and Marketing Services,* offered by Executive Communications, 411 Lafayette Street, New York, NY 10003; phone: (212) 831-3147. The latest edition, issued in September 1994, is priced at $75.00, plus $3.00 handling.

Employee leasing may be another solution. In the uncertain economy of recent years, this service has grown rapidly—from only 5,000 leased employees in 1983 to some 700,000 in 1990. *Megatrends 2,000* author John Naisbitt has predicted that by the end of the century, 1 of every 15 workers will be leased. Leasing works this way: You pay the leasing service a fee. It rents employees to you and assumes all personnel functions. Leased executives fill positions ranging from middle to top-level senior management.

How to Pay for It

You can pay for freelance work in any of several ways. To some extent, the nature of the work may dictate the most practical method of payment.

Creative Work

If you and the writer or art director expect to work together for some time, you may set up a **retainer fee** under which any reasonable amount of work, or a reasonable maximum, will be done. An alternative is an hourly rate—but make sure you both agree on an estimate of the time it will take to complete a given assignment. Another way to go is with the **per-assignment fee,** in which you agree to pay a certain amount regardless of how slowly or how quickly the freelancer gets the work done. In this case, the wise freelancer will quote a price high enough to protect himself or herself from your spending more time than expected on meetings and revisions.

Some writers may propose to negotiate a **percentage deal,** in which they earn a percentage of the gross income from sales that result from their work. This arrangement is more likely to be proposed when the writing is for direct response advertising, where results can be attributed to specific advertising vehicles. Or the copywriter offers to work up an assignment "on spec" (on speculation), with the promise of payment based on results. Percentage arrangements can be troublesome. Suppose you and your copywriter get into a debate over some headline or the handling of copy. You insist on having it your way, which is, after all, your prerogative. The ad doesn't pull as well as expected. Now your writer can tell you he or she has lost money because of your change. Or suppose, on the other hand, the ad pulls better after your change. What does that do to your relationship?

The fact is that if you have taken pains to find a capable copywriter or art director, a percentage deal is not a good deal for either side. A talented creative person will do good work for a fair price regardless of final results, and final results—even in direct response—are the consequence of many variables. If a particular piece of creative work brings in astounding sales, you can always present an appropriate bonus to the genius freelancer. But you'll be wise to avoid the percentage deal, even if the writer brings it up.

Production Work

When you hire a freelancer to produce a television or radio commercial or a printed brochure, you may agree to pay him or her **out-of-pocket costs** plus a markup. That means the markup is added to an itemized bill for everything from studio rental and raw videotape to typesetting, artwork, blueline proof, and printing. Or you may pay the out-of-pocket costs plus an hourly rate for the freelancer's services.

Other Counseling

Market planning and other management tasks may call for working out a negotiated fee to be paid to the freelancer regardless of the time spent. This is similar to the retainer or the per-assignment fee.

In considering any arrangement for paying an hourly rate, pay close attention to the factors discussed later in this chapter under "Independent Contractor Status."

How Much to Pay for It

Pay for freelance talent varies widely. In major advertising centers—New York, Chicago, Los Angeles, San Francisco—those who are talented and well experienced can earn more than $100 an hour or more than $500 a day. Younger, less experienced writers and art directors in smaller cities may work for as little as $20 an hour—maybe even less. The spread in freelance pricing is wide.

If you are talking about an assignment fee, you may offer the freelancer a set price—$300 or $500, say, for writing or designing an ad, commercial, or flyer and for following it through production. Or you may ask the freelancer to come up with a price. You may want to get competitive bids from two or three writers or artists.

To give you an idea of prices for freelance art directors' services, you may want to order a copy of *Pricing & Ethical Guidelines* from the Graphic Artists Guild, 11 West 20th Street, New York, NY 10011; phone: (212) 463-7730. The guide is updated biannually. Cost is $24.95 plus shipping and handling, which is $4 if sent to you book rate via U.S. Postal Service, $5 if sent via United Parcel Service (UPS).

Don't forget that your freelance art director will bill you for out-of-pocket expenses, such as photostats or typesetting, and is entitled to add a 15 percent handling fee. The art director or copywriter, like the producer, can be expected to pass along such charges as long-distance phone calls or photocopying and may charge you for auto mileage if trips are a necessary part of the assignment.

Another possible arrangement on price: Agree with your freelancer to set the fee for a day's work at 1 percent of what a year's salary would be for the same job. Again, you will have to check around among people you know to see what advertising agencies and other advertisers in your corner of the world are paying their staffers. Generally speaking, salaries are higher in New York than in Charlotte, North Carolina, or Portland, Oregon, or points in between. *Note:* If you start paying a freelancer 1 percent of a year's salary for a day's work and the work load becomes five days a week, you will find yourself paying out a year's salary in less than six months. Better to have hired staff or brought in an ad agency. This is one more reason for working up a marketing plan that tells you where you are going and what your needs will be.

How to Judge It

How do you know if the work you are getting from your freelancer is any good?

That question can be asked about the work of not only your freelancer, but also any advertising agency or in-house staffer you hire. The question has no easy answer.

One way to judge is to apply the criteria listed at the end of Chapter 4. Beyond the virtues and sins listed there, the question of whether copy or design is good or bad is often a matter of *taste.* The ability to recognize good taste in advertising develops from some years of looking at ads and commercials and observing what seems to be lasting work—work that advertisers repeat and repeat because, obviously, it is producing results. At the same time, you can probably also observe more advertising that is in bad taste. You can train yourself to appreciate good, effective advertising even if you yourself are not the one creating it. And, if in doubt, you can put pretesting and posttesting research to work (see Chapter 5).

Beyond that, trust your professionals. If you have screened your freelancers carefully before hiring them, reading their sample ads and reviewing their commercial reels more than once and probing thoughtfully into the background of the creative work, then respect the work they recommend for production.

Warning: On the other hand, do keep your good-judgment eyes open. In the past, art directors have recommended and advertisers have approved and publications have printed ads in which a reply coupon calling for name and address was printed entirely in reverse type—white typography and white lines on black background. Countless ads carry coupons too small for normal handwriting. "Artsy" or "designy" ads that make clever visual patterns more important than the direct relationships between headline, copy, and illustration are more valuable as examples of an artist's self-expression than as communication tools.

Independent Contractor Status

When you hire freelancers, you want to be certain to distinguish them as **independent contractors.** If you rely on such workers, there is a good chance that Uncle Sam may knock on your door to demand proof that these people are not actually employees. Concerned that companies are trying to avoid paying payroll taxes by misclassifying workers, the IRS has dramatically increased its payroll audits in recent years. At the same time, the government suspects that freelancers may fail to report all of their self-employment income. Given these concerns, the IRS prefers to collect taxes directly from employers.

State auditors are also looking closely at freelance arrangements. Most states want to make unemployment insurance available to as many people as possible, so they look for opportunities where freelancers can be reclassified as employees.

From your point of view, of course, the independent contractor gives you an advantage. You can save maybe one-third of such traditional payroll costs as insurance, pension, and other benefits—not to mention the related administrative work.

What distinguishes a freelance independent contractor from an employee? In one leading case, the test was described as follows:

> The distinction between an employee and an independent contractor has been said to be the difference between one who undertakes to achieve an agreed result and to accept the direction of his employer as to the manner in which the

CHECKLIST FOR DETERMINING INDEPENDENT CONTRACTOR STATUS

The following checklist was adapted from a list by the Tax Division of the AICPA. The greater the number of YES answers, the more likely companies will meet the IRS test for independent contractor status.

	YES	NO
Has an independent contractor agreement been signed?	________	________
Does the contract state that the company has no right to control the work performed?	________	________
Does the company prepare a letter upon completion of the contracted work stating that terms of the agreement were met?	________	________
Does the contract state that the independent contractor cannot be fired if contractual obligations are met?	________	________
Is the independent contractor paid by the job rather than by the hour?	________	________
Is the independent contractor viewed as a skilled worker?	________	________
Does the contractor set his or her own hours of work?	________	________
Does the contractor furnish his or her own tools?	________	________
Does the contractor perform the work off-premises?	________	________
Does the contractor negotiate payment with the company?	________	________
Does correspondence consistently refer to the worker as an independent contractor?	________	________
Does the company refrain from dictating the sequence in which work is to be performed?	________	________
Is the contractor free to work for several firms or persons simultaneously?	________	________
Does the independent contractor have business cards, advertise or in other ways promote his or her business?	________	________
Is there evidence that the company's competitors treat similar workers as independent contractors?	________	________
Does the company refrain from requiring the contractor to submit oral or written reports?	________	________
Does the company refrain from sending supervisors or others to check on work progress?	________	________
Does the company refrain from requiring independent contractors to do the same type of work as its regular employees or that is part of day-to-day operations?	________	________
Is the company refraining from providing training to the independent contractors?	________	________
Does the contractor have the right to:		
• hire and fire assistants	________	________
• treat assistants as his or her own employees?	________	________

Source: American Association of Advertising Agencies Bulletin, No. 4970. *Management Matters,* vol. 2, no. 4. January 13, 1993. Reproduced by permission.

result shall be accomplished, and one who agrees to achieve a certain result but is not subject to the orders of the employer as to the means which are to be used.[1]

Several factors help to determine whether an employer-employee relationship exists:

- *The nature of the services performed.* Generally, employees perform work continuously, whereas an independent contractor signs on to do a specific job. Independent contractors should be receiving assignments from more than one client and should be dealing directly with them.
- *Method of remuneration.* An employee usually is paid a fixed wage on a weekly or hourly basis, whereas an independent contractor usually receives a total sum for his or her work.
- *Office, overhead, and other business expenses.* Independent contractors should be able to substantiate real office or home office expenses and other business-type expenses. If an individual pays his or her own travel and entertainment expenses, provides his or her own secretarial help, and does not receive a paid vacation or other benefits, independent contractor status is suggested.
- *Other factors.* Independent contractor status is further suggested if the individual hired (1) has an obligation to furnish equipment, material, or tools; (2) has agreed to furnish a product as opposed to labor; (3) does the work on premises other than those of the person by whom he or she was hired; and (4) is not required to observe set hours.[2]

For a handy checklist that can help you determine whether your arrangements with freelancers meet the IRS test for independent contractor status, see the box "Checklist for Determining Independent Contractor Status" on page 95.

For a second checklist, to make doubly sure you are clear on whether a freelancer is an employee or an independent contractor, pick up IRS Publication 937: *Employment Taxes and Information Returns.* A portion of this publication is reprinted on page 97.

Put It in Writing

Not only to protect yourself against the IRS but also to maintain your goodwill and avoid any misunderstandings with your freelancers, it's a good idea to draw up a simple contract or **letter-of-agreement** that spells out your arrangement. Make sure it includes:

- A description of the nature of the assignment or work to be done
- Agreement that confidentiality of information provided to the freelancer will be maintained
- Restriction against the freelancer working for your competition during the period of the agreement, or longer, if you so desire and are willing to continue some remuneration for the length of the agreement
- A clear statement on ownership of ideas as **work-made-for-hire**
- A provision for indemnification against any problems or legal actions resulting from the work

1. American Association of Advertising Agencies Bulletin, No. 4600. March 22, 1990, 1. Adapted by permission.
2. American Association of Advertising Agencies Bulletin, No. 4600. March 22, 1990, 2. Adapted by permission.

Employee or Independent Contractor?

An employer must generally withhold income taxes, withhold and pay social security and Medicare taxes, and pay unemployment taxes on wages paid to an employee. An employer does not generally have to withhold or pay any taxes on payments to independent contractors.

Common-law rules. To help you determine whether an individual is an employee under the common-law rules, the IRS has identified 20 factors which are used as guidelines to determine whether sufficient control is present to establish an employer-employee relationship.

These factors should be considered guidelines. Not every factor is applicable in every situation, and the degree of importance of each factor varies depending on hte type of work and individual circumstances. However, all relevant factors are considered im making a determination, and no one factor is decisive.

It does not matter that a written agreement may take a position with regard to any factors or state that certain factors do not apply, if the facts indicate otherwise. If an employer treats an employee as an independent contractor and the relief provisions discussed earlier do not apply, the person responsible for the collection and payment of withholding taxes may be held personally liable for an amount equal to the taxes that should have been withheld.

The 20 factors indicating whether an individual is an employee or an independent contractor are:

1) ***Instructions.*** An employee must comply with instructions about when, where, and how to work. Even if no instructions are given, the control factor is present if the employer has the right to control how the work results are achieved.

2) ***Training.*** An employee may be trained to perform services in a particular manner. Independent contractors ordinarily use their own methods and receive no training from the purchasers of their services.

3) ***Integration.*** An employee's services are usually integrated into the business operations because the services are important to the success or continuation of the business. This shows that the employee is subject to direction and control.

4) ***Services rendered personally.*** An employee renders services personally. This shows that the employer is interested in the methods as well as the results.

5) ***Hiring assistants.*** An employee works for an employer who hires, supervises, and pays workers. An independent contractor can hire, supervise, and pay assistants under a contract that requires him or her to provide materials and labor and to be responsible only for the result.

6) ***Continuing relationship.*** An employee generally has a continuing relationship with an employer. A continuing relationship may exist even if work is performed at recurring although irregular intervals.

7) ***Set hours of work.*** An employee usually has set hours of work established by an employer. An independent contractor generally can set his or her own work hours.

8) ***Full-time required.*** An employee may be required to work or be available full-time. This indicates control by the employer. An independent contractor can work when and for whom he or she chooses.

9) ***Work done on premises.*** An employee usually works on the premises of an employer, or works on a route or at a location designated by an employer.

10) ***Order or sequence set.*** An employee may be required to perform services in the order or sequence set by an employer. This shows that the employee is subject to direction and control.

11) ***Reports.*** An employee may be required to submit reports to an employer. This shows that the employer maintains a degree of control.

12) ***Payments.*** An employee is paid by the hour, week, or month. An independent contractor is usually paid by the job or on a straight commission.

13) ***Expenses.*** An employee's business and travel expenses are generally paid by an employer. This shows that the employee is subject to regulation and control.

14) ***Tools and materials.*** An employee is normally furnished significant tools, materials, and other equipment by an employer.

15) ***Investment.*** An independent contractor has a significant investment in the facilities he or she uses in performing services for someone else.

16) ***Profit or loss.*** An independent contractor can make a profit or suffer a loss.

17) ***Works for more than one person or firm.*** An independent contractor is generally free to provide his or her services to two or more unrelated persons or firms at the same time.

18) ***Offers services to general public.*** An independent contractor makes his or her services available to the general public.

19) ***Right to fire.*** An employee can be fired by an employer. An independent contractor cannot be fired so long as he or she produces a result that meets the specifications of the contract.

20) ***Right to quit.*** An employee can quit his or her job at any time without incurring liability. An independent contractor usually agrees to complete a specific job and is responsible for its satisfactory completion, or is legally obligated to meke good for failure to complete it.

Form SS-8, In doubtful cases, the facts will determine whether or not there is an actual employer-employee relationship. If you want the IRS to determine whether a worker is an employee, file Form SS-8, *Determination of Employee Work Status for Purposes of Federal Employment Taxes and Income Tax Withholding,* with the District Director.

Source: Department of the Treasury Internal Revenue Service Publication 937 (Rev. Nov. 93).

- A clear statement on ownership of materials produced by the work (for example, keylines or mechanicals, videotapes or audiotapes, etc.)
- Agreement that both parties will comply with applicable laws and regulations
- A definition of charges (out-of-pocket or otherwise) that are to be allowed, including how extra charges resulting from changes shall be treated
- Schedule of meetings, presentation of draft copy or layout, completion of final copy and art, production, delivery, etc., including how delays or cancellations shall be treated
- A statement that the freelancer, as an independent contractor, is not entitled to participate in employee-benefits programs
- A joint-severability statement making it clear that, if any part of the agreement is struck down, the rest of it survives
- Acknowledgment that the freelancer is free to work elsewhere at any time, with the exception of the restriction against working for competitors (see third bullet)

One final word. The IRS is serious. If it can prove that you have misclassified employees, it can penalize you the amount that you should have withheld or as much as double that amount. If it can prove a crime was committed, the sentence may be a fine of $100,000 on the corporation or a year in prison for the executive responsible or both.

Summary

If you do not set up an advertising department or hire an ad agency, you may hire freelancers to handle your advertising program. Check their references and the quality of their work carefully.

Freelancers in advertising are of four types: moonlighters, who are employed in full-time jobs but who are seeking additional income or challenge; retirees, who may have taken early retirement but find it boring; the temporarily unemployed, who have been laid off because of various changes in business conditions; and full-time freelancers, who prefer to work in the home studio or office. In addition to creative talent, you can find freelance help in most of the functions of the advertising industry.

Where do you find them? Through networking with other advertisers, media people, and suppliers; in the Yellow Pages and the specialized *Directory of Independent Advertising and Marketing Services;* and through employee-leasing services.

Payment may be in any of several arrangements, including retainer fee, hourly rate, per-assignment fee, out-of-pocket costs plus markup, and negotiated fee. Think twice before you agree to percentage deals, as they can be troublesome.

How much to pay is a tough question. The answer depends on where you are located and on the freelancer's background and experience. Rates may vary from $20 or less to $100 or more per hour.

Judging the work of the freelancer can be based on the fairly hardball criteria listed as The Seven Heavenly Virtues and The Seven Deadly Sins at the end of Chapter 4 and on a more softball criterion: taste. Aside from developing your own ability to recognize good taste in advertising, you can put pretesting and posttesting to work to provide unbiased judgment. Beyond all that, trust your professionals.

It is important to distinguish your freelancers as independent contractors. The IRS suspects that companies are trying to avoid paying payroll taxes and other deductions by misclassifying workers. State auditors are equally stringent. Review the nature of the services performed, the method of remuneration, the substantiation of office and other business expenses, and various other factors on a thorough checklist (see Checklist for Determining Independent Contractor Status, page 95).

To be safe, always sign a letter of agreement with your freelancer that clearly spells out your arrangement.

PART THREE

WHERE DOES ADVERTISING GO? HOW DOES IT REACH THE PUBLIC?

Advertising often looks very simple. But...the problems are as many and as important as the problems in building a skyscraper. And many of them lie in the foundations.

— Claude Hopkins, *Scientific Advertising*

CHAPTER EIGHT

Look at All the Paid Media

KEY TERMS

Advertising Research Foundation
Association of Business Publishers, Inc.
Audit Bureau of Circulations
bulletins
cable interconnects
circulars
circulation
clutter
cost-per-thousand
exposure
freestanding insert
frequency
gross rating points
horizontal publications
media vehicles
out-of-home media
output-ready
pass-along reader
reach
run-of-print
spot radio
spot television
spread
trade advertising
Traffic Audit Bureau
transit advertising
vertical publications

Nothing can be more important to the success of your advertising program than a thorough understanding of what media is and how it operates. This chapter concentrates on what media is. The next chapter details how it operates: media planning and media buying.

Why is understanding media so vital? Because if you do not understand it, you cannot answer the key question you should always be asking about your advertising: Is it working? If you are not doing media right, your competition is probably getting calls from media sales people who have ideas on how to do it better.

Doing media right means making the best-informed decisions you can on where to spend your advertising dollars. To help you make media decisions, you want quantitative data about the various media that put advertising before the public. All the major media categories are served by independent auditing organizations that validate the **circulation** figures of specific media. This audited third-party circulation data becomes the basis for determining the cost per thousand exposures, the cost per rating point, and statistics on the reach and frequency of advertising exposures. **Reach** is advertising jargon for the total audience that sees or reads or hears some portion of your message at least once in a given period. **Frequency** is the number of times your message is exposed to an average household or person over a given period. **Cost-per-thousand** (CPM) is how much it costs you to expose your message to a thousand people. A rating point is 1 percent of the total target audience. **Gross rating points** (GRPs) are the aggregate number of rating points in your total advertising schedule. You can also get a GRP figure by multiplying reach times frequency (see Chapter 9 for more on this).

For many decades, the media categories have been newspapers, magazines, radio, television (broadcast and, more recently, cable), and out-of-home. These categories are still your primary concern, but you should also be aware of the dramatic changes taking place in media. New technologies have broken up the established patterns by which these media reach their audiences. In the past, radio and television signals reached their audiences over the air waves, newspapers and magazines moved through the mail or were hand-delivered, cables carried nothing but telephone calls, and out-of-home advertising referred to those signs by the side of the road.

Now such distinctions are rapidly becoming out-of-date. Cables bring all kinds of video and audio channels into the home. And telephone cables now do more than simply carry voices from place to place. Through modems and phone lines, com-

PAID ADVERTISING MEDIA: TRADITIONAL VERSUS 1990s

Traditional

- Print: Newspapers and magazines
- Broadcast: Television and radio
- Outdoor: Billboards and paints

1990s

- Print: Newspapers and magazines
- Broadcast: Television and radio
- Outdoor: Billboards and paints
- Cable: Multiple television and multiple audio
- Direct Broadcast Satellite (DBS)
- Broadcast Satellite Sound (BSS)
- Multichannel Local Distribution Service (MLDS)
- On-line print: Newspaper and magazine features via modem
- Out-of-home: Radio; television in classrooms and waiting rooms, on air flights, etc.; posters on grocery shelves, ski lifts, golf carts, etc.

puters are downloading newspaper and magazine articles, which can be printed out or read off the screen. Television is found on airplanes and in the waiting rooms of everything from bus depots to auto dealers' service departments. And out-of-home advertising is everywhere, from shopping carts to golf carts. See page 104 for a summary of the many changes that have taken place in advertising media.

The fact is that the day of mass markets and mass audiences has gone. Audiences are splintered and segmented and fractionated. They read, listen to, and watch many media categories and countless media vehicles within the categories. Most of the **media vehicles**—individual advertising media, such as a specific magazine or radio station—are narrowly targeted. You can take advantage of this to target your prospects and customers precisely.

What Do Your Customers See? What Do They Hear?

Broadcast and cable media—both television and radio—are oriented more to the small business retailer than to the small business that is selling business-to-business—with perhaps one exception: the business-to-business advertiser who uses radio commercials during the morning and/or evening commute to reach executives traveling to and from work.

Television and radio commercial time is sold on either a network or a "spot" basis. Don't even think about network. If you are a customer for network—in which your commercial appears in a regional or national hookup of stations transmitting the same program at the same time—you are too big to consider yourself a small-business advertiser.

Television

Television is known as a prime medium. It delivers its message to practically everyone. It presents your message in sight, sound, action, and color. You can target your market by geography and by television program. You can identify your audience by sex and age, as well as by where they live. But your targeting is somewhat limited. It is hard, for instance, to reach the sophisticated, better educated, upscale consumer, who watches less television than the others do.

When you buy **spot television,** you can select exactly when you want your message to be delivered. You may not always get the time you want, however, because there is only a certain amount of time available—in most cases, 9 to 15 minutes per hour—and there is considerably less time available during network prime time, when breaks for local spot advertising come in between programs.

Cable television gives you more flexibility and tighter targeting to specific audiences. The cable subscriber is younger, better educated, and enjoys a higher income level than the average viewer of traditional television. But cable is in only about two-thirds of all television homes in the United States, so you have to make sure your cable salesperson gives you precise information on the channel's subscribers.

Retail and other local advertisers are spending approximately $1 billion annually in spot cable television, and this num-

RADIO AUDIENCE
Monday-Sunday, 6 A.M.-midnight

Group		Weekly Reach	Average Daily Time Spent Listening (hours:minutes)
Persons	12+	95.7%	3:13
Teens	12-17	95.7%	2:13
Men	18+	95.5%	3:24
	18-34	96.4%	3:27
	25-54	96.6%	3:27
	35-64	95.9%	3:20
Women	18+	95.8%	3:16
	18-34	97.7%	3:20
	25-54	97.2%	3:13
	35-64	96.4%	3:13

Source: Fall 1992 Arbitron National Database. Based on total population.

ber is rapidly growing. One of cable's big advantages is that you can target your best prospective customers on a local zip-code basis, giving you much greater effectiveness than broadcast television offers. And **cable interconnects** can enable you to run commercials in small geographic areas.

If you are a retailer, spot television and spot radio can reach the younger generation of customers, who do not read newspapers as their parents did. You have to avoid being lulled by the security blanket that print—mostly newspaper advertising—has always been to the retailer, especially since newspaper advertising salespeople work hard to keep retailer business. Some 63 percent of retailers surveyed recently said they had weekly contact with newspaper salespeople, while only 26 percent saw their television salespeople that often. Not only that, but the survey disclosed that 40 percent of retail advertisers could name their newspaper salespeople, but not even 1 percent could name a single television salesperson. Even so, a 1993 study of retailers disclosed that, out of nine media categories, retailers regarded spot television as their most important advertising medium, considering it twice as important as cable advertising.

Radio

Spot radio is extremely efficient for reaching almost any target audience. You can find a wide variety of programming formats, each with its own crowd of loyal listeners. There are stations specializing in talk shows, soft rock, heavy metal, country music, classical music, African-American and Hispanic culture, sports, news. The number of different audiences that radio reaches is countless, but all radio stations know their own audiences—their ages, sex, income levels, and life-styles.

Radio production is inexpensive and fast, so you can get out a message quickly when you want to. Radio advertisers can get a new commercial on the air in as little as 12 hours after realizing they need a fresh message. Most stations are eager to help increase your radio buy's value by providing such merchandising aids as contests and on-the-air promotions, or by sending one of their broadcasting personalities to appear at your sales meeting, store opening, or other promotional event.

But radio is a background medium. It is not intrusive. People are usually doing something else while they are "listening" to the radio. This inattentiveness means that your creative people must work hard—*really* hard—to get your message across. See the box on 104 for more detailed information on the nation's radio audience.

What Do They Read? Print

Newspapers

A long-standing belief among local retail advertisers is that if you run ads in the newspaper, you are a legitimate business. You gain a trust or credibility that you can get almost no other way.

What are some of the other advantages of advertising in a newspaper?

- *You reach your audience quickly.* Your newspaper ad captures most of its total audience in a single day—typically, about 60 percent of the households in a given market area. If you are pushing a promotion or running an offer that is timely, you gain strong urgency.
- *Readers go to newspapers.* Newspapers bring news to readers, true. But readers pick up newspapers, more than any other medium, in search of sales, classified ads, and coupons.
- *You get flexibility.* You can schedule your ad (in a daily) on any day, in the section where a particular type of reader—sports fan; business person; homemaker; auto buff; film, music, or theater devotee; etc.—is likely to see it, in any size from a two-page **spread** down to an inch or two of a single column.
- *You can get in quickly.* Lead time is short. In most papers, you can get your ad in within two or three days, and if you're in a real hurry, you can often get in within 24 hours.
- *Your computer can talk to theirs.* Not in every case, yet, but in markets where newspapers enjoy circulations from 50,000 to 100,000, a little more than one-third of the papers accept electronic transmission of advertising material that is **output-ready** (that is, digital ads in final form prepared on Macintosh or IBM PCs or compatibles). In markets where circulation is under 25,000, only about 13 percent of the papers have equipment that accepts output-ready copy.

Tip: If your business, like most retailers' today, is computerized, and if you are buying newspaper space, check to see what electronic equipment your paper has. If you are mailing or hand-delivering your insertion orders and ad copy, and if your newspaper is letting you handle it this slow, old-fashioned, costly and less efficient way while they are computer literate, someone is not in tune with the times.

How about disadvantages?

- *Newspapers get stale fast.* The first advantage above is also a disadvantage. Newspapers are thrown out in a day or two.
- *Your selectivity is limited.* You can target certain groups or types of readers, but that's about it. Some other media—cable television, with its zip-coding, or narrowly targeted radio—can give you closer aim on your prospects.
- *You are caught in a cluttered and unpredictable environment.* You don't know what news headline or other ads may be competing with your ad for attention.
- *Your creativity may be hampered by reproduction limits.* Compared to other print media, newspaper reproduction is poor. In most papers that have gone to **run-of-print** color, for instance, the quality of reproduction is still far behind that pioneered by the national newspaper *USA Today.* If, like many a retailer, you are of a mind to stop running sale ads and start creating a real relationship with your customers, you may want to think hard about whether newspaper advertising can give you enough of a quality look to improve your image.

Some interesting facts about how small businesses feel about newspapers were discovered in a 1992 survey sponsored in 24 markets across the United States by the International Newspaper Marketing Association. The association wanted to find out how well newspapers were serving small and medium retailers—such as those selling apparel, furniture, groceries, jewelry, sporting goods, eyewear and optometric services, and interior design services—and what the stores needed that newspapers were not providing. Among the findings:

- Newspapers continued to raise prices even though the retailers' sales could not support the increases.
- Service was declining in newspaper advertising departments.
- Small retailers did not get the respect and concern given larger customers.
- Asked what improvements they sought, the largest number of respondents said they would like newspapers to give them more marketing information.
- The average retailer used nearly five media, including newspapers, during the course of a year.
- Cable and direct mail were gaining advertising dollars from retailers; among those using cable, 40 percent used it more than they had the year before.
- Small retailers wanted assistance with layouts and other creative work.
- Asked what media they depend on the most, 62 percent of the retailers named newspapers. Direct mail was next, with 11 percent, while television and radio each were named by only 6 percent.
- But when asked to rate the media by performance for their type of business, 41 percent said newspapers were excellent or very good, while 38 percent said this of direct mail; 30 percent, television; 22 percent, radio; and 15 percent, cable. Only 14 percent cited Yellow

Pages display ads, and 5 percent referred to magazines as excellent or very good performers.

You may find that you can buy space for less in a "shopper," or freely distributed newspaper, than you can in a paper that has paying subscribers. The reason for the price difference is that customers who have to pay for a paper are assumed to be more likely to read it. Papers that simply arrive in the mail or on the doorstep are more likely to be tossed out unread. Some subscriber papers, on the other hand, have a way of distributing some sections—the weekend magazine or feature section, for example—as a free mailing to every residential address in a given zip code, usually with several **freestanding inserts (circulars** for retailers, usually shopping centers, malls, or discount or department stores). You may be charged a premium if your ad appears in a section getting such a boost over the paper's paid circulation or, thanks to the paper's advertising manager, it may be manna from heaven.

Consumer Magazines

If your target audience is divided into specific segments with special interests and characteristics, you can't beat magazines as the category for reaching them. Selectivity is the word. You can aim your advertising right at your prospect. Business-to-business advertisers find this advantage even stronger in business-to-business publications (see next section).

Listed below are some of the advantages that magazines offer in attracting, informing, and persuading an audience:

- *You use rifle, not shotgun.* Because you can buy so many sizes and shapes of advertising units in so many thousands of magazines, you can target and reach your audience with greater cost efficiency and much less waste than you can with other media.
- *Readers are with you.* People buy magazines for their specific editorial content. Your advertising message can be tailored to that editorial environment, creating a synergistic effect.
- *Readers are involved.* Since they have an interest in the magazine's editorial content, readers are apt to be interested in pertinent advertising material. In many cases, the reader has bought the magazine in order to look for relevant advertising.
- *They look more than once.* Readers return to magazines. They save back issues. Your ad gains repeat exposure. Unlike television or radio, magazines give readers time to think about your ad. Unlike newspapers, your ad does not wrap up tomorrow's garbage.
- *You can look good and be creative.* Four-color reproduction is top quality in most magazines. Two-color or black-and-white are excellent in almost all. You can write long copy if you have a complex story to tell. You can bind in preprinted inserts or spread your ads over several pages or include coupons or even product samples.
- *You can go where your geography takes you.* Many national publications will sell you advertising space that goes only into print runs destined for specific states, smaller regions, metropolitan areas, or test markets—thanks to zip-coding. That

means your target audience sees you in a prestigious national magazine. There are also regional and city magazines that cover your local market. And newspapers in larger cities publish magazine supplements, usually on Sundays, that are edited for local readers.

- *You can target demographically, too.* Upper-income households, specific age groups, men or women, life-styles, hobbies, business classifications—whatever market characteristics you want to designate, you can usually find a magazine that is directed at your target.
- *Your ad gets pass-along readership.* Anyone who reads a publication but was not the buyer (nor a member of the buyer's family) is a **pass-along** (or secondary) **reader.** Such readers count in the total readership of a magazine. Doctors' and dentists' offices are full of pass-along readers. Most magazines reach at least three or four readers per copy.

Do magazines have any disadvantages? Yes, here are the most obvious:

- *You can't be in a hurry.* Many monthly magazines demand as much as 90 days of lead time to reserve ad space or to get your production material in—or both. If you're dealing with fast-changing market conditions, this long lead time can make it tough. Weekly news magazines that offer regional advertising buys (such as *Time, Newsweek, U.S. News & World Report, Sports Illustrated*) work much tighter schedules, often handling ad insertions quite close to publication dates.
- *You can't be as intrusive as television.* No sound. No action. No jingles or MTV excitement. If you insist on yelling and screaming your message, you have to find a way to do it in print.
- *To stand out, you have to be creative.* In a typical magazine issue, at least 50 percent of the content is advertising. This **clutter** is considerably more intense than that on television or radio. Your ad must get attention in a busy environment.
- *Your readership has to build up.* Total readership of a magazine accumulates. If it is a weekly, it takes about five to six weeks to reach its entire audience. If a monthly, the period can be at least nine weeks—maybe longer. For statistics on audience accumulation see table on page 111.

In the magazine world, you can find literally thousands of publications. Some 600 of them submit statistics faithfully to the independent **Audit Bureau of Circulations** (A.B.C.), an organization of advertising agencies, advertisers, and publishers. Its purpose is to determine correct circulation figures and distribute them to all interested parties. If you are thinking of running your advertising in any magazine, check with its salesperson on whether it is audited by the A.B.C. If it isn't, proceed with caution, for you will have no guarantee of how many readers the publication really does reach.

Or Do They Concentrate on Trade and Technical Journals?

Business-to-business publications are specialized, edited for and directed to people who make purchasing decisions, or influence them, for their companies. More than 3,000 such business publications reach

AUDIENCE ACCUMULATION
Percent of Total Audience Reached
by Weekly and Monthly Magazines

	Weekly	Monthly
Week 1	60%	40%
Week 2	80	60
Week 3	92	65
Week 4	98	70
Week 5	100	75
Week 8	—	89
Week 9	—	100

Source: "What Every Account Executive Should Know About Media," American Association of Advertising Agencies. Reproduced by permission.

three broad categories of reader:

- *Trade.* These are retailers and wholesalers. *Note:* Just to confuse you, people in the business often use the term trade press to mean all of the business press. Technically, they are wrong. **Trade advertising** is intended to appeal to wholesalers and retailers.
- *Industrial.* These readers are the ones who specify, directly or indirectly, the purchase of industrial goods.
- *Professional.* Doctors, lawyers, accountants, nurses, teachers, etc., read these magazines, a number of which are published by the professional societies to which such readers belong.

In addition, some 300 farm publications are edited specifically for readers who grow, produce, or deal in agricultural products.

Think of business publications as either of two types:

- **Vertical publications.** These magazines cover specific industries or areas of interest, such as medicine, banking, electronics, construction, real estate, chemistry—even advertising.
- **Horizontal publications.** These deal with job functions, such as purchasing, human resources, bookkeeping and accounting, sales management, or research and development.

What are the advantages and disadvantages of business-to-business magazines over other media? See the listings above under "Consumer Magazines." The comments on targeting and cost effectiveness, editorial environment, pass-along **exposure,** accumulation of audience, and flexibility in creative work as well as in geographic and demographic targeting are all applicable to business-to-business publications. So are the comments on disadvantages: You can't be in a hurry, the medium is not intrusive, you need real creativity to break through the clutter, and it takes time to accumulate total readership.

Can business-to-business advertising be

linked directly to sales and profits? A major study by the independent **Advertising Research Foundation** (ARF) and the **Association of Business Publishers, Inc.** (ABP) proved that it can. The study tracked actual sales and found that business advertising produces significantly more sales than would occur without it. The study also revealed that business-to-business advertising

- Generates higher profits
- Results in awareness of your company's name and image
- Positions you against your competition
- Provides your prospects with information on your product
- Introduces new products and technological advances
- Draws attention to sales promotions and special programs
- Pulls inquiries
- Opens the door for your salespeople to make calls

What are you spending now on a sales call? Experts say the cost per call has reached more than $250. Compared to that price, the cost of business-to-business advertising is a bargain—probably the most cost-efficient and effective way you can find to get your sales message to a specific industry (vertical) or type of function (horizontal).

How About When They Leave the House?

As its name implies, **out-of-home media** includes whatever advertising is seen outside of the home—giant billboards on which posters are pasted; painted signs (known as **bulletins**); **transit advertising** (in airport, bus, and train waiting rooms; on railroad and subway platforms; on bus shelters; on the inside and outside of buses, trains, and taxicabs); displays in shopping malls; and blimps, airplane tows, and skywriting.

What makes this advertising medium distinctive and worthwhile is that it has the lowest cost-per-thousand (CPM) of all the media.

But that is not the only advantage your out-of-home advertising enjoys. Other advantages:

- *You get high reach.* In one month, your ad is seen by 60 to 90 percent of the total population. Seventy percent of that total reach is gained in the first week.
- *And you get high frequency.* Typically, your ad is exposed to each viewer from 6 to 30 times a month.
- *Your audience cannot avoid it.* No zapping, tuning out, or leaving reading material unopened. Out-of-home is simply there, working for you all day, every day, as your audience passes by. If you use color dramatically, it is big and bold and hard to ignore.
- *You can be selective.* No medium is more geographically discriminating. You can target a region, a metropolitan area, a tight core area, or literally a point-of-sale location. Your advertising can be located close to a shopping center (if not right in it), a dealership, a restaurant, etc., so it is likely to be the last sales message your prospect sees before going inside the shopping center, dealership, or restaurant. Demographic selection is good, too. Ethnic, economic, or special-interest

groups? Out-of-home can be placed to reach any specific audience.

- *You look big and impressive.* No other medium can give you such a giant display area.
- *Your audience is upscale.* In terms of location, most out-of-home advertising skews toward the upscale, in positions where the demographics of education, income, etc., are toward the upper end of the range.
- *You can be highly creative.* The opportunities are limited only by the imaginations of your creative people. Extensions can be built outside the normal dimensions of a painted bulletin. Moving parts and unusual lighting can be devised. Inflatable attachments can add drama. Designs can be three-dimensional.

The out-of-home media category has its disadvantages, too. Among them:

- *You can't always get what you want.* From market to market, you will find substantial variations in availability. If the only board in the perfect location at the busiest intersection is already under long-term contract—tough luck.
- *The demographics are limited.* You can't be selective by age and sex, because in our free world anybody can drive or walk past your advertising. The one exception is public rest-room advertising (yes, there is such a thing), in which you can target either men or women.
- *Don't expect a high attention level.* Exposure in usually involuntary—and extremely brief. For most people who see your poster or paint, the experience lasts only six to eight seconds.
- *Your creative people must face certain challenging limitations.* The big one? Copy. Experts who have tested readership or pass-by attention spans say the *maximum* number of words on a successful billboard or painted bulletin is seven. For *all* out-of-home media, copy must be concise and succinct, and design must be bright and colorful, bold and uncluttered. Longer copy can work only on cards inside buses, trains, and subways, where your audience usually has some time to read.
- *The law may hamper you.* Some states and cities have passed laws prohibiting or limiting certain types of out-of-home advertising. Be sure the salesperson lining up your ad tells you of any restrictions before your creative people waste time and money coming up with marvelous ideas that break the rules.

Out-of-home is carefully measured by an independent organization called the **Traffic Audit Bureau** (TAB). Since 1933, it has authenticated circulation data for the outdoor media. TAB audits traffic, or opportunities for exposure, near outdoor displays. It uses a count of adults aged 18 and over so that you can compare this medium to others. Note: For some unexplained reason, it is the general impression among salespeople in the out-of-home media that retailers don't care about audits of this medium. If you are a retailer, you should care—unless you have no interest in getting what you paid for.

The last word about out-of-home advertising is one word. As with real estate, the three most important things are location, location, location.

Sometimes They're Already Looking for You

The Yellow Pages has a specific function. While the other media work to get attention for the product or service you are selling, build awareness of it, and start your customer moving toward you, the Yellow Pages is a directional medium. It tells a customer exactly where he or she can find your product or service. Some 54 percent of people who open the Yellow Pages have one or more firms in mind, but 31 percent of them end up choosing another firm, while 46 percent of those using the Yellow Pages have no firm in mind at all. This means that you have a great opportunity to sell to prospects who may not be familiar with your company, and you have a chance to get business from the nearly one-third of Yellow Pages users who were thinking of going to one of your competitors.

Like other media, the Yellow Pages offers certain advantages:

- *Your message can appear in a variety of sizes and shapes.* You choose from more than 50 types of ads, ranging from full pages down to simple listings in bold typeface. This gives you an equally wide range of costs. Some directories offer four-color units.
- *You can target markets.* Directories are published according to geographical markets. In some, you can zero in on zip codes and neighborhoods.
- *You can pinpoint consumer interest.* You have some, but not all (see disadvantages below), demographics in hand. By carefully choosing the heading under which you list your business and place your advertising, you select an audience life-style. Usage of the Yellow Pages by people with upper incomes is higher than general usage.
- *You can't get better credibility.* Everyone usually assumes that information in the Yellow Pages is absolutely reliable.

Are there any disadvantages? Yes. You should be aware of these:

- *You're in for a year.* Once your ad appears, you cannot make any change for 12 months. Whatever you said in that ad is set in concrete—phone number, address, product line and description, listing of services you offer, location of stores—until next year's book is delivered to telephone customers.
- *You can't target the demographics.* Age, sex, ethnic or racial group, profession, income—the Yellow Pages cannot distinguish one user from another in any of these ways. The breakup of the Bell Telephone System and deregulation of the telephone industry, however, have resulted in the rise of independent, specialized directories that are oriented to women, senior citizens, and others.
- *You have to obey the rules.* Yellow Pages publishers seem to set more regulations than the government. They dictate. You listen.
- *You have no control over placement of your ad.* In other print media, you usually can specify where your advertisement is to appear. Not so here, except for deciding under which heading you want to be listed. You and your competitors sit side-by-side on the page—an important challenge for your creative people.

If one of your objectives is to keep your customers loyal, and if another is to help insure the effectiveness and cost efficiency of your other advertising, you should take some care to put the Yellow Pages to good use. When a customer is presold or preconditioned, the information and direction he or she finds in your ad can reinforce the customer's commitment to your business.

How Local Advertisers Choose and Use Media

If yours is a local business—if you are a retailer or other merchant—you may be wondering at this point, How do local advertisers choose and use their media? Three advertising professors carefully studied local markets in Georgia and Wisconsin in search of the answer to this question. They defined local advertisers as companies, businesses, or establishments that primarily served consumers rather than other businesses; operated in a single, relatively narrow geographic area (such as a single county); and had recently used one or more advertising media. Respondents had to be individuals at the businesses who made the decisions about advertising spending and use of media. Businesses using advertising agencies or other consultants were excluded.

The findings? Daily newspapers were used by 77 percent of the advertisers, and

LOCAL ADVERTISERS' MEDIA USE: WHAT MEDIA ARE YOU CURRENTLY USING TO ADVERTISE YOUR BUSINESS?

			How long have you used this medium?				
Medium	**Percent using (%)**	**Percent* of budget (%)**	**Under 1 year (%)**	**1-2 years (%)**	**3-5 years (%)**	**Over 5 years (%)**	**Unsure (%)**
Daily Newspapers	77	43	6	12	14	56	11
Yellow pages/phone directories	58	5	3	10	12	68	7
Radio	57	27	13	12	12	54	9
Weekly newspapers	46	26	8	11	18	54	9
Direct mail	45	19	8	17	14	55	6
Magazines	26	17	10	32	16	32	10
Word of mouth	26	15	2	8	8	73	8
Cable television	21	16	18	28	18	30	7
Broadcast television	20	23	24	8	21	42	5
Billboards or outdoor	16	23	23	23	3	40	10
Shoppers/coupon books	14	12	19	19	23	31	4
Specialty ad media	48	14	1	3	4	10	81

*Share of budget devoted to the medium by those who reported using the medium.

Source: Nowak, Glen J., Glen T. Cameron, and Dean M. Krugman. "How Local Advertisers Choose and Use Advertising Media." *Journal of Advertising Research.* November/December 1993, 43. Reproduced by permission.

COMPARISON OF MEDIA USE BY TYPE OF BUSINESS: WHAT MEDIA ARE YOU CURRENTLY USING TO ADVERTISE YOUR BUSINESS

	Business category			
Medium	**Autodealer (%)**	**Restaurant (%)**	**Consumer services (%)**	**General merchandise (%)**
Billboard/outdoor	40.0	12.5	23.3	12.0
Broadcast TV	46.7	31.3	20.0	16.0
Cable TV	60.0	12.5	23.3	16.8
Daily paper	93.3	81.3	80.0	74.4
Direct mail	33.3	37.5	50.0	46.4
Local magazine	20.0	25.0	40.0	23.3
Radio	86.7	81.3	50.0	51.6
Shoppers/coupon books	20.0	12.5	30.0	8.8
Weekly paper	20.0	68.8	53.3	44.0
Yellow pages/phone directories	73.3	56.3	80.0	51.2

Source: Nowak, Glen J., Glen T. Cameron, and Dean M. Krugman. "How Local Advertisers Choose and Use Advertising Media." *Journal of Advertising Research*. November/December 1993, 44. Reproduced by permission.

they devoted 43 percent of their ad budgets to newspaper advertising. Among 56 percent of these advertisers, the newspaper habit was more than five years old (see table on page 115).

Different businesses used different media. Auto dealers used billboard/outdoor, and they and restaurants used radio heavily. Consumer service firms were the heaviest users of shoppers and coupon books, while general and specialty merchants used these media the least (see table above).

Is cost the deciding factor when local advertisers make media decisions? No. The study found that audience reach—how many people see your ad—was the most important consideration. Second came the ability of the medium to target a specific audience. Total cost to produce and buy the ad was third, ahead of a number of other factors. But notice that auto dealers put the ability to generate immediate traffic ahead of everything else. For a list of other decision making factors, see the table on 117.

Local advertisers rated daily newspapers and direct mail as tops in the ability to reach the target audience and in cost effectiveness (see page 117).

Daily as well as weekly papers captured the honors when it came to the helpfulness of salespeople in planning an advertising campaign.

LOCAL ADVERTISERS' ASSESSMENTS OF MEDIA DECISION-MAKING FACTORS*

Media decision-making factors	Grand mean	Auto	Restaurant	Consumer services	General merchandise
Number of people who will see your ad	4.75	4.8	4.5	4.7	4.8
Ability to target/reach specific audiences	4.56	4.5	4.6	4.3	4.6
Total cost to produce and purchase the ad	4.51	4.2	4.9	4.5	4.5
Number of times your ad will appear	4.23	4.4	4.1	4.2	4.2
Ability to generate immediate store traffic	4.19	4.9	3.7	4.1	4.2
Ability to reach the entire market	3.87	4.5	3.4	4.0	3.8
Program or editorial environment the ad will appear in	3.86	3.9	3.8	4.4	3.7
Cost per thousand people reached	3.67	4.1	3.0	4.1	3.6
Advertising rate discounts or incentives	3.65	3.4	3.6	3.7	3.7
Quality of media sales representatives	3.57	2.6	3.4	3.9	3.6
Availability of audience research	3.44	3.5	3.1	3.4	3.5
Extent your competitors use the medium	2.77	3.0	2.7	2.7	2.7

* On a scale of 1 to 5, with 5 being very important, please rate the following media-selection factor.

Source: Nowak, Glen J., Glen T. Cameron, and Dean M. Krugman. "How Local Advertisers Choose and Use Advertising Media." *Journal of Advertising Research*. November/December 1993, 43. Reproduced by permission.

LOCAL ADVERTISERS' EVALUATIONS OF FIVE LOCAL MEDIA*

Advertisers' evaluations	Daily newspaper	Direct mail	Cable TV	Weekly newspaper	Yellow pages
Ability to reach the target audience	3.35 (2)	3.44 (1)	2.60 (5)	2.88 (3)	2.78 (4)
Cost effectiveness	3.13 (2)	3.30 (1)	2.38 (5)	2.75 (3)	2.49 (4)
Helpfulness of sales representative in planning your advertising campaign	3.26 (1)	2.63 (3)	2.33 (5)	2.91 (2)	2.47 (4)

*On a scale of 1 to 5, with 5 being better performance, please rate the media for the following.
Rank appears in parentheses for comparison with other media for each item.

Source: Nowak, Glen J., Glen T. Cameron, and Dean M. Krugman. "How Local Advertisers Choose and Use Advertising Media." *Journal of Advertising Research*. November/December 1993, 44. Reproduced by permission.

Summary

To know whether your advertising is working well, it is important to understand media. Its categories have been changing rapidly from the traditional print (newspapers and magazines), broadcast (television and radio), and billboards of yesterday. In addition to these traditional media, there is now a wide variety of cable, computer network, cable television, and out-of-home media.

Spot television commercials broadly present your message with sight, sound, action, and color, but you are somewhat limited in targeting your audience demographically. Cable television gives you more flexibility and allows tighter targeting to specific audiences. Both spot television and spot radio reach younger audiences, who are less likely to read newspapers than their parents were. Spot radio can be targeted with great efficiency. Production for it is inexpensive and fast, so you can get your message on the air in as little as 12 hours. But radio is a background medium—its "listeners" are usually doing something else at the same time, so your creative work must be of breakthrough quality.

Newspaper advertising bestows legitimacy on any business. This medium offers many advantages—the urgency of the news medium, flexibility in targeting specific readers, short lead time, electronic transmission of production materials. Its disadvantages include short life (a day or two), a cluttered environment, and poor reproduction quality.

Consumer magazines enjoy much longer life and have pass-along readers. Your advertising message can hit an audience bull's-eye with little waste, in an editorial environment that helps create synergy. Reproduction is excellent. But you have to cope with long lead times (often as long as 90 days), and magazines lack the intrusiveness of television as well as its immediacy, with total readership taking from six to nine weeks to accumulate.

Trade, industrial, professional, and farm magazines make up the business-to-business publications category of media. They are either vertical (edited for specific industries or areas of interest) or horizontal (edited for job functions). Advantages and disadvantages are like those of consumer magazines.

Out-of-home media has the lowest cost-per-thousand advertising impressions of all the media, with high reach and frequency. Geographically, it is highly selective, but demographics are limited. Attention level is low. Advertising's creative people are challenged by the constraints of out-of-home, such as having to limit copy on billboards and painted bulletins to seven words. Also, some cities and states have passed laws prohibiting or limiting out-of-home advertising.

The Yellow Pages' value as an important advertising medium is that it gives you the opportunity to grab prospects who were thinking about going to your competition. Because directories are published by geographic markets, you can target your market closely. But you cannot target demographically, and you cannot change your advertising message for a full 12 months.

A major study of how local advertisers choose and use media disclosed that 77 percent used daily newspapers, spending 43 percent of their ad budgets in them. But different types of businesses used different media—for example, auto dealers were heavy users of out-of-home, and restaurants were heavy users of radio. When it came to choosing media, advertisers stated that reach and the ability to target a specific audience were more important than the cost of producing and placing the advertising.

CHAPTER NINE

Planning and Buying Media

KEY TERMS

ABC
ADIs
Arbitron
ASRs
avails
bleeds
BPA
cancellation date
checkerboard ad
circulation audit
circulation rate base
closing date
CMSA
controlled circulation
co-op advertising
dayparts
DMAs
editorial environment
8-sheets
flight
gutter
insertion date
insertion order
interconnects
island ad
make good
media service
media vehicles
Nielsen
package
pink sheets
plants
PMSA
postride
preprinted insert
preride
rate cards
rotation
run-of-paper (ROP)
sales rep
showings
SMSAs
SRDS
30-sheets
tight market
trafficking
verbal order
white sheet
YPPA

Before you think about the specifics of planning and buying media, think about some broad principles. The people who are selling you media are selling intangibles. That is always a tough sale, and it makes for salespeople who are eager and insistent. Be sure they provide you with plenty of support for the decisions you have to make. The really smart media salesperson knows that he or she has a certain responsibility to help make your business successful. So he or she will contribute factual information about the audience and the market served by the particular media vehicle, to help you spend your advertising budget efficiently.

Getting an advertiser's media efforts organized and accomplished is both an art and a science. It is done by individuals in small businesses, by large departments of people in major advertisers and ad agencies, and by independents called media consultants or media services. Whoever does it, these basic steps are involved:

- *Media planning.* The media person figures out where your advertising should run. He or she looks over all the **media vehicles** that might be useful and recommends the most effective environment for your message. He or she also tries to determine how to spend your advertising dollars most effectively and backs up recommendations with solid statistical data and other information.
- *Media buying.* The media person negotiates for advertising time or space, trying to get the most favorable buys in terms of programming or environment and price. He or she is also the steward of the buy, checking that the advertising runs as planned and bought.

Media Planning

The first question in media planning is, What are the media objectives? A statement answering this question should head your plan. The objectives must deal with three key questions: What is the target audience you want to reach? When do you want to reach them? Where should you advertise in order to reach them?

Target Audience

You have to decide whether your target is the person who actually uses your product or service, or someone who buys it for someone else to use, or someone who makes the decision to buy but does not make the purchase, or someone who influences the purchase but does not actually make the decision or the purchase. And is your target someone who is already your customer or only a user of the type of product or service you are selling?

Suppose you are a retailer selling athletic shoes. Your target may be the young mother who bowls or plays tennis (the user), the young father who buys shoes for his Little Leaguer son (buys for someone else to use), the older father who lets his daughter buy expensive ski boots (makes the decision but does not personally make the purchase), or the high school coach who tells her players what type of shoes to buy (influences but does not make the decision or the purchase). Right there you have four different target audiences, each of whom you want to make aware of your store as well as attract them to it.

But that's not all. It is important to define your target audience in terms of demographics and psychographics. For example, your targets for your athletic shoes might be described as follows: Married adults, 25 to 54. Teenagers. Household size: 3+. Household income: $40,000. Education: high school +. Life-style: athletic. Influencer, guidance authority.

Period of Concentration

Think about seasonality. When, in the course of a year, are people most likely to spend money for your product or service? How long does it take them to make the decision? If you are selling athletic shoes, you probably have a run on kids' sneakers in the early spring and ski boots in the late fall. Decision time, in either case, is very short—probably almost immediate. But if you are a travel agent, you want to sell packaged skiing vacations at Rocky Mountain or Swiss resorts a good six to nine months ahead, so people have time to make such major vacation decisions. And you'll want to target those with the most upscale demographics.

Geographic Strategy

Where should your advertising run? If you are a retailer, you know how wide an area you draw from. But what if you want to extend your radius? Or open a branch or add to your chain? If you make a product and notice you have a lower-than-average market share in some markets, what should you do to correct this? To deal with problems like these, you need to advertise in regional as well as local media. And, as always, you need to plan carefully to be sure your dollars are spent reaching the right audience.

Communication Considerations

Think about what levels of advertising you need in order to accomplish your objectives. And think about which is more important—reach or frequency? Your thinking is bound to be influenced by a number of factors, including

- How much pressure your competition is putting on you.
- How complex a message you need to get across. (Can you make your point in 30 seconds on radio or television or in seven words on a billboard, or do you need several blocks of copy in a newspaper or magazine ad?)
- How often people buy your product or service.
- Whether or not promotions are planned.

If your competitors are spending far more on advertising than you are, for example, you'll be smart if you limit reach and build frequency so that a small audience sees your advertising often rather than a large audience seeing it rarely. But if you are introducing a new product or store or launching a big promotion, you want to expand your reach so that more and more people become aware of you.

Reach, Frequency, and Other Jargon

It helps if you know the vernacular of the advertising business (see also Chapter 8). Reach is the percentage of your target audience that sees or reads or hears some portion of your message one or more times in a given period—usually four weeks. Frequency is the average number of times within that period that your message is exposed to an average household or individual. A rating point is 1 percent of the total target audience. Gross rating points (GRPs)—the sum of all the rating points for your individual ads—tell you how much total advertising weight you are getting for your money. One of the best descriptions of how reach, frequency, and GRPs are interrelated is shown in the table on page 124.

In other words, for the same amount of money, you can devise a media plan that reaches more of your target audience less often, or fewer of your target audience more often.

REACH, FREQUENCY, AND GRPS

The following example should help to define these terms as well as illustrate how they interact. To simplify these concepts, let us assume a total population (universe) of ten prospects. Let us also assume that the advertising schedule consists of commercial spots after five programs (A through E). The Xs in the grid indicate which spots were viewed by each of the prospects.

	Program									
Prospect	**A**		**B**		**C**		**D**		**E**		**Frequency**
1	X		—		X		—		X		3
2	—		—		—		X		—		1
3	X		—		X		—		X		3
4	—		—		—		—		—		0
5	X		X		X		X		X		5
6	X		—		X		—		X		3
7	—		—		—		—		—		0
8	—		—		—		—		X		1
9	—		—		—		X		—		1
10	—		X		X		—		X		3
Rating	40	+	20	+	50	+	30	+	60	=	200 GRP's

Four prospects (1, 3, 5, and 6) were exposed to the spot at the end of Program A. The rating for A was 40 (four out of ten). Adding the ratings for each of the five programs yields a total of 200 gross rating points (GRPs). For the total schedule, eight out of ten prospects (all except 4 and 7) were exposed to the message at least one time. That translates to a reach of 80 percent. The average frequency is found by dividing the gross rating points (200) by the reach (80), resulting in an average frequency of 2.5 times. Assuming a finite budget, an increase in reach will usually result in lower frequency, and conversely, the higher the frequency, the lower the reach.

Source: Brivic, Allen. *What Every Account Executive Should Know About Media.* American Association of Advertising Agencies. Adapted by permission.

Media Vehicles

Your next step is to determine which types of media the plan should include—print (newspapers? magazines?), electronic (radio? broadcast television? cable television?), out-of-home (billboards? painted bulletins? transit? skywriting?), or Yellow Pages? For each type of media you are considering, round up facts and information to help you decide which ones will be most effective. Following are things to look for when choosing specific vehicles within a medium. Although compiling all this information may seem like an enormous chore, once you've done it, you'll have an extremely valuable file for future reference.

Print

Information you should know about magazines and newspapers.

What You Want to Know

Editorial content. What subject areas are regularly covered? Who is the target audience of the publication? Are there features or special sections pertinent to your advertising interests?

The editorial staffing on business-to-business magazines is important. You want to know how many full-time editors the publication has and whether they have engineering or chemical or other professional degrees. And are they producing the kind of editorial content that will take the reader to the page where your advertisement appears?

Many business-to-business publications are owned by business or professional associations. Their **editorial environment**—or to use a stronger word, slant—may convey the bias or point-of-view of the association.

Publication schedule. How often are issues published? Daily, weekly, monthly, quarterly? If daily, is it A.M. or P.M.?

Date on sale. Weekly newspapers are usually published on Wednesday or Thursday, reaching newsstands on the publication date and subscribers by mail the next day. Magazines are almost always on sale or in the mail several days before the date of issue. If timing is a key factor in your advertising, this information may be important in your decision on whether to use a particular vehicle.

Circulation rate base. Advertising rates are based on the publication's paid circulation. Usually this is less than the actual circulation of the paper or magazine, with the difference viewed as a bonus. Some publications declare a *guaranteed* circulation rate base. All other things being equal, always go for the guarantee.

Note: Some publications, both consumer and business-to-business, are distributed by **controlled circulation** to selected individuals, households, or business places at no charge. Their rate cards should disclose whether the circulation they claim is audited or unaudited.

Circulation audit. Reputable publications make sure that independent audit services verify their circulations. (See section Where to Find Out about It on 127-128 for names of such services.)

Regional flexibility. Some national magazines, particularly the weekly news and sports publications, print different ads for distribution to newsstands and subscribers in different geographic regions. Many a small business gains the prestige of appearing in a big-league environment by buying such space.

Using zip-code distribution, many newspapers deliver feature sections *gratis* to nonsubscribers. Some papers are moving beyond zip-coding to deliver specific messages to specific households. The Long Island, New York, daily *Newsday* offers advertisers 130 different delivery zones. It can deliver a retailer's catalog only to its subscribers who hold the store's charge card. Papers nationwide—in Chicago, Houston, and Miami, among others—are developing similar capabilities.

Sizes of advertising units. Newspapers accept almost any size from a full page (or a two-page spread) down to a column wide by a few inches deep. Most papers set a minimum depth; if you want something smaller, you advertise in the classified ads. Magazines go from spreads and full pages—which may include **bleeds** that let your illustration extend to the very edge of the page, without a margin—down to single-column width and one- or two-inch depth.

Ad placement. Often—and sometimes for a premium price—you can position your ad where you want it, rather than accepting **run-of-paper (ROP)** positioning. In newspapers, you may want to be in the business, sports, entertainment, or homemaking pages.

City or regional magazines will sell you the inside front or back cover; the outside back cover; or positions within or opposite specific features that get high readership, such as the table of contents. Specific placement is available in most business-to-business magazines, too. The national magazines that sell space to regional advertisers are less likely to offer these options, as the printing and binding process prescribes where the regional advertising has to fit in.

Some magazines accept unusual, attention-getting layout ideas, such as a **checkerboard ad** (you buy two quarter pages on the same page, positioning them at opposite corners, and editorial content fills in the other two quarters) or an **island ad** (you "float" a quarter-page ad in the center of a page of editorial copy). Newspapers don't like to get into such "designy" games. Generally, magazines and newspapers compose their pages from the bottom up, putting the largest ads in the lowest position on the page and piling smaller ads on top. Editorial material is almost always placed from the top of the page down; it may run down a single column on the left or right of the page, with advertising running either toward the **gutter** (the crease in the center of the publication) or out to the edge of the page.

Most publications accept **preprinted inserts** that are bound into the issue at the time of production. Most newspapers and some magazines accept freestanding inserts, which are not bound in but are placed within the issue for distribution.

Rates. All publications state their prices on **rate cards.** Many prices are negotiable. You can get a wide variety of discounts: frequency, volume, group, corporate, etc.

Closing date: space. Every publication has an absolute last day on which it can accept an order or reservation for advertising space; otherwise, a publication would never know how many pages to plan or how much editorial content to produce, and it would never get printed by the publication date.

Closing date: material. To get off the press on time, every publication also has an absolute last day on which it can accept advertising material.

Space cancellation date. Most publications name a date after which they will not accept cancellation of an order for space. If you change your mind or plans too late, you must pay for the ad even if you do not run it. Usually, the space closing date is also the cancellation date.

Coverage of your target audience. How many readers does the publication have within your target audience? If you have more than one target, which readers belong to your primary group?

Buyers or subscribers versus pass-along readers. Knowing how many of each the publication has will help tell you whether readers have a strong interest in it.

Cost-per-thousand (CPM). This figure is a strong indicator of how efficient the publication is against the target audience. Smart business-to-business marketers who see a meaningful part of a publication's circulation going to their target markets are glad to pay the CPM based on total circulation.

Vital signs. You want to know whether the publication is here to stay, so you can be confident it will support your advertising. Is its circulation trending upward or downward? How about the revenue it takes in per advertising page—is it up or down? And renewals of subscriptions?

Where to Find Out About It

The sales representative who calls on you. Space salespeople at magazines and newspapers know a lot more than you think about the market served by their publications, about what your competitors are doing, about your category of business. They certainly know the ins and outs of their rate cards. Don't hesitate to put them to work helping you.

Rate cards. You can get much of the information you are looking for by studying rate cards—usually not cards but leaflets or folders put out by the publications. They include answers to many of the questions posed in the "What You Want to Know" listing above.

SRDS. Standard Rate & Data Service puts out directories that list advertising prices and production requirements for periodical, television, radio, and transit advertising. Circulation, ad sizes, closing dates, regional advertising opportunities, current rates, as well as policy on rates, description of the editorial environment and the publication's market and intended audience, names of salespeople—all are included in the SRDS "bible," which is updated every month. The reference desk at your local library may have it. Or contact Standard Rate & Data Service, 3004 Glenview Road, Wilmette, IL 60091; phone: (312) 256-6067.

ABC and BPA. The two most important services that audit the circulation of publications are the Audit Bureau of Circulations (ABC) and the Business Publications Audit of Circulation (BPA).

ABC puts out its Publisher's Statements, better known as **pink sheets,** twice a year. These contain information compiled by the publisher of each magazine. The Audit Report, or **white sheet,** is published annually and contains audited details on the two previous Publisher's Statements. Information included on each audited publication:

- Circulation of an average issue (regional editions included)
- Circulation issue by issue
- Circulation by county size and state
- Number of subscribers and single-copy sales
- Number of new versus renewal subscribers
- Number of copies sent to subscribers after expiration of subscription
- Rate base in effect during the statement period
- Comparison of circulation in pink sheet Publisher's Statements versus white sheet Audit Report, to show trend
- Annual trends for past five years

BPA's analysis of the circulation of business and trade publications comes out twice a year. Magazines are classified by market group. Among the data reported in the audit for each issue of a publication are its total circulation, its geographic distribution, and the occupations of its subscribers.

Audited circulation statements show you where magazines are concentrating their reach and to what extent they saturate their markets. Make sure that salespeople representing magazines and newspapers provide you with either ABC or BPA statements. The exceptions? If the publication's pages carry more than 75 percent advertising content (that is, have less than 25 percent editorial) or if the publication is new and not yet eligible for an audit, in which case you want to make sure it will be audited as soon as possible.

Important addresses, phone and fax numbers:

Audit Bureau of Circulations
Communications Department
900 N. Meacham Road
Schaumburg, IL 60173-1968
(708) 605-0909
Fax: (708) 605-0483

Business Publications Audit of
Circulation, Inc.
270 Madison Avenue
New York, NY 10016
(212) 779-3200
Fax: (212) 725-1721

Electronic

Information you should know about radio and broadcast and cable television.

What You Want to Know

Programming. What are the media vehicles covering? News, talk shows, soap operas, situation comedies, sports, cartoons, cooking shows, do-it-yourself shows, dramas, top-40 music, country-and-western music, or what else? Your television or radio spots are going to be seen or heard within some program or between two programs, depending on what **dayparts** you buy into. When you consider buying time on any television station, you want to know what the environment will be.

Media people divide the broadcast day into parts. Advertising rates vary according to these dayparts (see the following tables).

Times of dayparts may vary slightly depending on the stations and markets. Prime time is when television viewing is at its peak. You want to know who is tuned in at the various times during which you are thinking of buying spots.

Ratings. The rating is a measurement of who's watching or listening. It is the percentage of total households or the population able to receive a program—those owning television sets or radios—who are actually tuned to a particular program or station at a specific time. If, for example, 7 percent of all men aged 18 to 49 in a specific geographic area are watching or listening to a particular station or program at a specific time, the station or program has a 7 rating.

How much you pay for a spot depends on the rating of the program it appears in or adjacent to. Spots tend to cost less if your goal is simply to reach broad-based targets such as households or adults aged 18+. Demand for spots that do not focus on a target group is low, so the station charges less for them. If you want to reach a specific target group—teens, say, or adults 18 to 25—you pay more. It's a supply-and-demand situation, too, because there is only so much commercial time per hour or program. That's why spots in Super Bowl broadcasts cost a small fortune—the rating is tops, the reach is tops, a frequency of only one spot in the game can deliver millions of viewers. For this opportunity, advertisers are willing to pay top dollar.

Market size also affects rating. The rating is based on the percentage of the pos-

TELEVISION DAYPARTS

Daypart	Eastern Time*
Early morning	6:00 A.M. — 9:00 A.M.
Daytime	9:00 A.M. — 3:30 P.M.
Early fringe	3:30 P.M. — 5:30 P.M.
Early news	5:30 P.M. — 7:00 P.M.
Prime access	7:00 P.M. — 8:00 P.M.
Prime time	8:00 P.M. — 11:00 P.M.
Late news	11:00 P.M. — 11:30 P.M.
Late fringe	11:30 P.M. — 1:00 A.M.
Late night	1:00 A.M. — 6:00 A.M.

*Slight variations may occur in central, mountain, and Pacific time zones.

RADIO DAYPARTS

Daypart	Time		
Morning drive	Sign-on	—	10:00 A.M.
Midday	10:00 A.M.	—	3:00 P.M.
Afternoon drive	3:00 P.M.	—	7:00 P.M.
Night or teen	7:00 P.M.	—	Sign-off

sible audience that is actually tuned in, but the total potential is obviously bigger in a big market, city, or metropolitan area, than in a small one.

Length of commercials. The standard commercial lengths today are 30 seconds and 15 seconds in most dayparts on television and up to one minute on radio. Longer commercials are sold by some stations in the late-fringe and late-night television dayparts and on night radio. The longer the commercial, the more you pay.

Scheduling. You face a number of choices as to when your advertising appears on television or radio. Which daypart is one decision, and if you want to reach more than one audience or market segment through more than one daypart, what are your options? **Rotation** is one: Your spots can rotate horizontally, scheduled in the same program or at the same time on different days of the week, or vertically, scheduled in different programs at different times throughout a specific day or days.

Scheduling in **flights** is another tactic: Your spots appear regularly for a period of 4, 6, or even 13 weeks; then they are not seen or heard for the same length of time; then they appear again for another flight. Research has proved that many viewers and listeners think they are continuing to be exposed to specific commercials that are scheduled in flights even during the in-between weeks when the schedule is on hiatus. Flighting helps give your advertising continuity. It is a practical way of stretching your budget to last as long as you want your campaign to last.

Stations like to **package** spots. They try to sell you spots on a number of programs and in several dayparts for a package price. The package is likely to include some high-rated spots and some low-rated ones. You can set a minimum rating, below which you don't want to buy any spots, but that limitation will probably raise the cost of the package.

Reach, frequency, GRPs. These elements have the same meaning in television and radio as in print advertising. In the electronic media, your spot commercials gather reach—the total number of people or households exposed to your message at least once—more quickly than they accumulate frequency. If you buy a broad variety of dayparts or program spots, you increase reach more quickly. If you spend the same amount of money but concentrate your effort in fewer dayparts or programs, frequency builds up more quickly. What you want is a combination of the two: spots in a variety of programs and dayparts but strong frequency within carefully selected programs. This will produce the optimum frequency among those viewers or listeners who are exposed to your schedule. In other words, you want to try to make sure that those whom you are eager to reach are the ones who get your message the most.

Rates. All broadcast and cable sales offices publish rate cards. Prices are often even more negotiable than in the print media. A **tight market** sends prices upward. Seasonal influences are strong: Christmas, graduation and wedding time in May and June, back-to-school. In print, the publisher can always add pages as orders for more advertising space come in. But in television and radio, station managers cannot increase the length of a day in order to meet demand. They can only charge more for the time they have available. Because of this, you may want to think about making one or more long-term buys that lock in favorable pricing over the length of the schedule.

Due date for buys. You want to set a deadline for buying time. The more lead time you have, the better—for two reasons. First, you need time to create and produce your advertising. If your copywriter and art director have not yet started the creative work, you'll need to build in time for this. You'll also need to plan for production time, which could be several weeks for television spots but which will be less for radio. Second, the timing of negotiations for buys in the electronic media, where fluctuations in market conditions are common, can be important in terms of your getting the best buys. If the market is tight, you'll be glad to have extra time for finding spots available that meet your objectives, or for analyzing alternatives in your total media plan. Allow at least six to eight weeks.

Delivery date for material. Stations like to have videotapes and audiotapes, or copy to be read "live" by radio announcers, on hand from 24 to 48 hours before airtime.

Make goods. Inevitably, a station will sooner or later run one of your commercials (or more than one) at some time other than the time you bought, or they will cut it short at its beginning or end or otherwise give you a faulty presentation. Rather than lose revenue by giving you credit on billing, the station will offer a **make good,** running the commercial correctly at a later time. If timing of your commercial was crucial to a promotion or sale, the make good may be useless and the error costly. Be sure to find out what the station's policy is on make goods.

Cable is different. Cable is a bunch of local systems that can be identified by zip code and that can be hooked together into networks called **interconnects**. "Hard" interconnects are systems tied directly by cable or microwave relay. All systems on the hard interconnect get their programming and commercials from a single head end. "Soft" interconnects do not have that direct operational connection. Your commercial in a soft interconnect is inserted at each participating system at the same time. You need to know where the specific systems are located and whether an interconnect is hard or soft. You can buy time either system by system, through an interconnect, or through a regional network.

Local cable television stations like to run rotation schedules. Why? In older systems and smaller markets, the technology doesn't permit them to put a specific commercial into a specific program—a limitation that is diminishing as cable grows. Also, with a number of cable channels offering homogeneous programming—all-news, all-sports, etc.—they are like radio or daytime television: Rotation is usually a more efficient buy than specific placement.

Where to Find Out About It

Station salespeople or reps. As in the print media, the salespeople at television and radio stations, or the stations' "reps" if the stations are affiliated with station representative firms, can be good sources of information on the markets they serve, on what your competitors are up to, on your field of business. Ask them for advice and help, but always keep in mind that they have a certain bias toward the stations they represent.

Rate cards. The answers to many of the questions raised in the "What You Want to Know" listing above can be found on station rate cards. The station salesperson or rep will be glad to go over the rate card with you.

Nielsen and Arbitron. Two major national firms, Nielsen Station Index (NSI) and Arbitron Television, issue quarterly reports —in November, February, May, and July— on local television viewing. Each service divides the continental United States into market areas based on viewing patterns. Nielsen calls them **DMAs** (for Designated Market Area). Arbitron calls them **ADIs** (for Area of Dominant Influence). Data on viewership is based on the demographics of age and sex in each market. Reports are also provided on ethnic viewing patterns, coverage by counties, viewership of local cable stations, and test markets.

Both services can provide their reports on computer tapes and diskettes. To help you tailor geographic and demographic information to your local market situation, they also offer data that combine local television ratings with product usage and other marketing data. Each service has numbers of reports and reference guides available.

Arbitron provides a similar service covering radio, with reports for each ADI covering 13 weeks of survey data by age, sex, and place of listening—at home, in automobile, or elsewhere—as well as the ethnic composition of the audience.

Another Arbitron service—Arbitron Cable Target Aid (ACTA)—provides cable systems with rating reports customized to the specific coverage area (for example, zip code) of a cable system or interconnect. Your cable salesperson or rep should be able to share this useful information with you.

Important addresses, phone and fax numbers:

Arbitron Television
142 West 57 Street
New York, NY 10019
(212) 887-1300
Fax: (212) 887-1390

Nielsen Station Index (NSI)
299 Park Avenue
New York, NY 10171
(212) 708-7500
Fax: (212) 708-7795

When You're Ready to Make the Buy

Having learned as much as you can about the television and radio vehicles that can be useful for your advertising, draw up a list of specifications that express the strategy of your plan. The list should include most, if not all, of the following:

- Your total budget to be spent in television and radio, broken out market by market if you are buying time in more than one
- Primary and secondary target audiences
- Geographic and demographic requirements
- ADI or DMA market list (whichever you prefer to work with)
- Rating service you prefer (Arbitron or Nielsen)
- Dates when you want to schedule flights
- Dayparts you prefer (or insist on)
- Budget breakdown by dayparts
- Gross rating points (GRPs) you seek for each daypart as well as total
- Reach and frequency you seek
- Length of commercials
- Starting date
- Any scheduling restrictions
- Your preference on make goods versus credits

Out-of-Home

Out-of-home media include posters, painted signs, transit, and displays.

What You Want to Know

The printed poster and the painted sign (or bulletin, in the jargon of the out-of-home advertising business) are the standard outdoor media vehicles. Firms that own billboards, painted bulletins, and other out-of-home media and that provide the printed sheets, paint, and construction are known as **plants,** OOH plants, or out-of-home plants.

Some of the things you should know in planning an out-of-home media buy:

Where they are. You can see out-of-home advertising media vehicles almost everywhere you go within or near Standard Metropolitan Statistical Areas (**SMSAs**). Four exceptions are Alaska, Hawaii, Maine, and Vermont. In some markets and states, tobacco and liquor advertising is not accepted.

Markets covered. Your advertising can be seen not only at specific locations leading into and out of markets, but it can also penetrate into ethnic neighborhoods, commercial or shopping areas where traffic is dense, and areas immediately adjacent to where your products are sold. Rotation can keep your messages changing and moving around a market. As mentioned earlier, cost-per-thousand (CPM) is lower than for any other medium.

You buy by showings. Posters (also known as poster panels) are sold in packages called GRP (Gross Rating Point) showings. A showing size is the degree of market coverage you get when you buy a given number of posters. It is not the actual number of panels you get. Rather, it is the number of panels you need to buy in order to gain a specific level of coverage in the market. For example, a #50 GRP showing will expose your advertising—in what is known as duplicated exposure opportunities—to 50 percent of the adult population of the market every day.

Reach and frequency. If you buy a #50 GRP showing of poster panels, in one month your advertising will reach three of every four adults in the market with a frequency of 15 times each. Though this does not give you narrowly targeted demographics or psychographics, it is unbeatable coverage.

How long is the run? Almost all units can be bought for 30-day periods. The exceptions are some displays in terminals and shopping malls, which are sold for three months, and painted bulletins, which (because painting and construction are expensive) are sold for one to three years.

Sizes and shapes. The basic units are:

- *Standard posters.* The best known are **30-sheets,** so named because it takes 30 printed sheets of paper to cover their 24-foot width by 12-foot height. Smaller **8-sheets** (5 feet high by 11 feet wide) can be found near stores, serving as excellent point-of-sale reminders.
- *Painted bulletins.* Permanent bulletins range from 10 feet high by 40 feet wide to 20 feet high by 80 feet wide. They can be embellished with two- or three-dimensional extensions outside the frames. Rotary bulletins (14 feet high by 48 feet wide) are usually repainted every four months, and copy is moved from one location to another every two months. This gives your advertising broad reach in the market.
- *Transit.* On the outside of buses, you can buy advertising space in a variety of sizes and shapes that give your advertising exposure to pedestrians and vehicular traffic. Size and exposure dictate the costs. In different markets, you will find taxi signs in different locations, some on rooftops, some at the rear. Inside buses, subway cars, and railroad commuter cars, you can buy rack position cards above the seats and windows or "hi-light squares" alongside doors and bulkheads. All provide reading time that is as long as the passenger's trip. Rail station and platform posters come in 1-sheet, 2-sheet, or 3-sheet sizes. Bus shelter, terminal, and mall displays and commuter clocks in subways and commuter stations usually are backlighted and may offer polarized "motion" effects.

Where to Find Out About It

Out-of-home is often the afterthought medium. Advertisers tend to think of it as an extra, to be used if any money is left over after the plans for print, television, and radio have been worked out. Small business advertisers, from pick-your-own-strawberries farms to local dairies to banks with a few branches in a 30-mile radius, use it effectively.

A number of sources can help you learn more about out-of-home advertising:

Salespeople and reps. As with the other media, those selling out-of-home should be able to give you detailed information on costs, on where postings are or will soon become available, on reach and frequency achieved by various showings, and on demographic coverage. They should also be candid about what your competitors are doing in this medium.

Rate cards. Every OOH plant has its rate card. These rate cards will answer many of the questions—about markets, what's available where, how GRP showings are priced—that you have.

The Buyer's Guide. The current statistics on rates and markets in the poster and rotary painted media are published twice a year, in April and September, in *The Buyer's Guide to Outdoor Advertising.* The guide includes three sections: (1) Areas of Dominant Influence (ADIs) by rank, with a list of OOH plants operating in those areas and a list of discounts shown on individual rate cards; (2) a state-by-state list of OOH plants, with rate and market information; and (3) an alphabetical listing of companies that offer rotary painted bulletins, with a second section organized by states and markets. The guide is available from:

Leading National Advertisers
11 West 42 Street
New York, NY 10036
(212) 789-1400
Fax: (212) 789-1450

Yellow Pages

What You Want to Know

Planning your advertising in telephone directories is a matter of matching the types and sizes of ads to your advertising objectives.

Basic objective. Your basic objective in buying space or listings in the Yellow Pages is probably to back up your other advertising's effectiveness and cost efficiency. A secondary objective may be to head off customers who might be thinking of switching to some other store or product or service.

Audience coverage. In this medium, which includes some 6,000 different directories, you are buying broad coverage that is segmented by geographic markets. You must decide on areas to be covered, depending on what kind of product or service you are selling, how near or far away your competitors are, and how far customers are willing to travel to come to you.

You can set up directory programs based on any of the commonly used market configurations: Standard Metropolitan Statistical Area (SMSA), Primary Metropolitan Statistical Area (**PMSA**), Consolidated Metropolitan Statistical Area (**CMSA**), Designated Market Area (DMA), or Area of Dominant Influence (ADI). Or you can match your Yellow Pages buys to zip codes.

Some basic national statistics may help you decide about your Yellow Pages advertising. The directories are used by 96 percent of all U.S. adults. Of that group, 57.8 percent refer to the Yellow Pages in a typical week—more than three times a week, on average. Among business buyers, 90 percent use the Yellow pages. Of them, 61 percent look in the Yellow Pages within a given week, at an average of five times a week (for business users, that's once a day).

Ad sizes. You can buy any size ad from a full page down to a line or two of boldface type. The choices include half and quarter pages, and two-column and one-column widths. When Yellow Pages users have been asked what influences them to choose an advertiser, 65 percent of those surveyed have said the size of the ad was the greatest influence. When ads for the same company were monitored for 243 working days, a simple two-line listing in boldface brought 128 calls, an ad one column wide by 1½ inches deep pulled 271 calls, and a quarter-page ad produced 746 calls.

If you are selling a product or service that is marketed nationally, or if your firm is a member of a national association, you may find that you can be listed in what are called trademark ads (TMs) in the Yellow Pages. Dealers, distributors, branches, and other outlets are listed under the big company's logo.

Tip: Think hard about whether you should advertise under more than one heading in the Yellow Pages. For example, if you are selling appliances, you should be under Appliances—Major—Sales & Service, Ranges & Stoves—Sales & Service, Dishwashing Machines, Refrigerators & Freezers, etc. This horizontal coverage is far more effective than vertical, or single heading, coverage. One large ad under a single heading does not usually constitute an effective Yellow Pages program.

Closing dates. These vary. But publication is annual. That means that when you start planning your Yellow Pages advertising, you may learn that you have just missed the closing and will have to wait a year to get in the next issue, or you may learn that publication is imminent and if you scramble like crazy maybe you will make it. Generally speaking, don't be surprised if it takes 15 to 18 months from initial planning through copy, design, and production to publication.

Where to Find Out About It

Consult the Yellow Pages. Within the first several pages of your local Yellow Pages, you will find plenty of basic information, including a map of your state showing geographical distribution of directories; a map of the primary distribution area for the directory you are looking in; and probably a full-page advertisement, run by the directory, that describes the benefits that advertisers get from it.

Rates and dates. Call the 800 number listed in your local Yellow Pages for information on rates as well as the deadlines for the next issues of area directories.

Yellow Pages Publishers Association (YPPA). To compare and evaluate coverage of various directories, check in with the national association, YPPA. It provides consumer demographics and Standard Industrial Code statistics on most of the 6,000 directories. It can also put you in touch with Authorized Selling Representatives (**ASRs**). The ASR functions as a clearing house, handling advertising orders and transmitting them to the appropriate publishers—if you want to buy an ad or listing in a directory not handled through the 800 number found in the beginning of your local Yellow Pages. To reach YPPA:

Yellow Pages Publishers
Association (YPPA)
820 Kirts Boulevard, Suite 100
Troy, MI 48084
(800) 841-0639
Fax: (810) 244-1323.

This completes the planning phase of your media plan. To recap briefly, for each of the basic media you expect to use, your media plan should describe

- Start and end dates, with the full sched-

ule on a spreadsheet
- Geographics, demographics, and pertinent psychographics
- Budget required to meet GRP goals, market by market
- For television and radio, daypart mix and GRPs by daypart
- Reach and frequency levels expected
- High and low limitations to be imposed on scheduling and ratings
- Policy on make goods versus credits for errors
- Due dates for insertion orders or for contracts for television/radio spots or OOH showings

Media Buying

For any medium you want your advertising to appear in, the process of media buying involves certain basic steps that are similar. They are (1) ordering, (2) trafficking materials for production, and (3) stewardship. We will first look at ordering the buy for the specific media: print, electronic, out-of-home, and the Yellow Pages.

Ordering

Print

Verbal order. At most newspapers and magazines, you can start on the phone, talking either with a rep firm or an advertising salesperson at the publication. Make it clear what insertion date and space size you have in mind and any positioning you prefer (in a newspaper: main news, sports, business, travel, entertainment; in a magazine: inside front or back cover, opposite table of contents). Get a firm quote on the rate and be sure to get three exact dates: (1) closing date for the insertion order, (2) closing date for materials, and (3) space cancellation date. In effect, your phone call reserves the space for you.

Insertion order. This written order must get there before the closing date. Send it addressed to a specific individual at the publication. If you have not already placed a verbal order, try to send the written order from seven to ten working days ahead of the closing date. The insertion order should include plenty of information: name, address, and phone number of the publication and of your company; **insertion date** (including A.M., P.M., or Sunday editions if it is a newspaper); size of space; cost of space as it was confirmed verbally; and any special instructions about the material (for example, placement of preprinted or freestanding inserts or of bound-in inserts or reply cards). The insertion order is a binding contract between you and the publication. Legally, you may revoke it up until the space cancellation date, but no later.

Electronic

Requesting avails. You start the buying process by getting in touch with the salespeople or sales representatives of appropriate stations to find out what is available or, to use the jargon of the business, to "request the avails." Let each salesperson know the basics you are thinking about: length of commercials, demographics and markets to be reached, flight dates, what dayparts or programs you want your spots to be in or adjacent to, the rating service (Arbitron or Nielsen) you prefer and the date of the rating report to be used in figuring costs, your preference on make goods versus credits, and any requests for merchandising help (such as counter cards that read, "As heard on station WXXX," or appearances by station talent at your promotional event). Finally, agree on a deadline for avails to be submitted to you.

Tip: If you tell the station salesperson how much budget you plan to commit to the buy, don't say what your GRP goal is. If you tell him or her what your GRP goal is, keep your budget information to yourself. Why? Put together, the numbers result in a cost-per-rating-point goal, which can establish a level beyond which the salesperson will feel no need to negotiate. Also, such information may be leaked to your competitors.

Evaluating avails. Each station's salesperson can be expected to call on you with a list of availabilities, probably in the form of a computer printout. It may itemize specific spots and propose packages of spots. The discussion will probably also cover the station's overall programming and performance in terms of ratings, its formats for commercial breaks in or between programs, promotional packages that may be offered, and trends and changes in the market. Don't hesitate to comment on any specific spots that you do not want or changes you would like to make in the packaging of spots.

Be sure to check out what you are being offered. Watch for programming changes since the last rating report, as they can critically affect the value of spots you buy. Check out the station's share of audience (that is, of all people watching or listening at a given time, the percentage tuned to the station) from the last two or three years' rating books to identify trends and the extent of any fluctuations caused by seasonal or programming changes. Think about the composition of the audience as well as the viewing trends among demographic targets and households during different rating periods.

After your evaluation, you may eliminate some avails—or some entire stations—because costs are too high or ratings are too low or you prefer the programming at other stations.

Negotiating the buy. Now you set out to get the lowest price you can for the most desirable collection of spots. When negotiating, try to find out whether the market for spots is soft or tight. If it is soft, you have the advantage. You can put together a buy on paper and name your price. A station may try a counteroffer, setting a price higher than your offer, or tell you to take their original price or leave it. Or you may suggest that the station improve the package offered by adding some bonus spots, by upgrading some of the spots in its package to higher-rated spots, or by giving you sponsorship of a segment of a program produced locally (such as the news). You may also agree to buy a number of flights all at the same time, as a way to leverage better value.

If the market is tight, you are at a disadvantage. To reach agreement, you may have to let the buy extend to include some softer buying periods, or you may have to spend more at a single station so that you can get more leverage, or you may even threaten—firmly but amiably—not to buy the station at all if it won't reduce its rates. Another lever is to buy only an immediate flight and keep future flights out of the negotiation, waiting until the market softens.

Finalizing the buy. In reaching a decision on which stations to buy, think about two factors: First, the more programs and stations you buy, the greater the total reach you get into your target audience. Each new addition brings different audiences into the total schedule. Second, the larger the share of your total buy a single station gets, the more likely it is to offer you lower prices.

When you are satisfied that you have negotiated the best buy you can in terms of schedule and prices, give the station rep or salesperson a verbal order. Within 24 hours, he or she should confirm it with a written confirmation or contract. Check the confirmation for any discrepancies from the verbal order, for it is a legal contract. It details your schedule's start date and length, number of spots per week, rotation (horizontal or vertical), specific time or more general daypart, name of program or daypart, demographics expected in your reach, and cost per spot or per package. The confirmation also specifies how make goods or credits are to be handled.

Out-of-Home

Take a preride. When you have worked up your plan, get in touch with the out-of-home plants you are considering and ask for availabilities, plus final, detailed information on costs, reach and frequency; demographics; and, in particular, what your competitors are doing. Then, before you commit to the buy, ask for a **preride.** This means the salesperson literally drives you around to view all locations to be considered in the buy. This can take time—a full day, maybe longer, depending on the number of locations and the distances between them. Any problem locations (such as too near a competitor's showing, demographic inadequacies, impending highway construction that will reduce pass-by traffic) should be discussed.

Negotiation. A plant may offer an extra month of posting as a bonus. Or bonus posters within your scheduled period. Because you are going into an intensive promotional period, you may agree to pay a premium to get a two-month showing on a key rotary that is usually contracted for four months. Upon agreement, your buy is frozen. You sign a contract.

Yellow Pages

In Yellow Pages advertising, you will find very little room for negotiation. You fill out an advertising order worksheet that is like an insertion order for print media. It itemizes the specifics of your buy. It is a legal contract. You sign it.

Trafficking Materials For Production

Print

Newspapers like to get all ROP (run-of-paper) materials two working days before the publication date. Insertions for Sunday are due on the preceding Wednesday or Thursday. Preprinted inserts and insertions for Sunday supplements are usually due from four to six weeks before publication. Magazines require materials from 30 to 90 days before publication date. Due dates vary, so make no assumptions.

Electronic

If your commercials are produced at one of the stations where you are buying time, that station should handle getting your tapes into its own traffic system so that they appear at the correct time on the schedule. The station may hand over tapes to you, in whatever quantity you need, for distribution to other stations. Or, if you are buying stations in other cities, it may agree to transfer your commercials via satellite uplink-downlink (the most convenient way to get this done), depending on the distance to other cities. Stations will charge you for duplicate tapes and for satellite transfers or shipping.

If your commercials are produced at an independent studio, its original bid or estimate for the job should include the production of duplicates in quantity as well as handling and shipping charges. You give the studio the list of stations in your buy.

In any case, your videotapes and audiotapes should be at stations at least 48 hours before airtime. Check your contracts for due dates.

Out-of Home

Your producer or art director prepares posting and painting instructions for the OOH plants. You should be sure to include any directions about special treatments—Day-Glo, unusual paints or colors, three-dimensional treatments or extensions beyond the bulletin frame, etc. Plants like to know where to expect problems.

Full instructions also go to the lithographer or other production house, with details on quantities to be sent to the OOH plant and deadlines that anticipate posting dates.

Stewardship of the Buy

Print

You want documentation that your advertising ran as scheduled. You can open your newspaper or magazine and tear out the page, but if you are running in several publications, it is better to make sure they are sending you tear sheets regularly. Keep them with other financial records as proof of performance. Check to be sure that tear sheets confirm that each ad ran on the date scheduled, in the correct size, and in the position you ordered. If your ad was pub set, review the copy and illustrations for accuracy. If you are running freestanding inserts, just keeping a copy does not prove that it was properly inserted in the correct number of copies. The publication should provide an affidavit as proof of performance.

Check on reproduction quality, too. If you are buying color, in newspapers or magazines, watch for poor color quality or printing that is out of register (a blurring or double image caused by one or more color plates not being lined up accurately).

If you find any discrepancies in quality, position, or dates, turn to your make-good policy. You may agree to the publication's running a make-good ad in a later issue, or you may accept an adjustment on your invoice.

Watch the circulation. To see that a publication is delivering its guaranteed rate base, check the Audit Bureau of Circulations (ABC) or Business Publications Audit of Circulation (BPA) Publisher's Statement for the period when your advertising ran. If the circulation was below the rate base, you are entitled to compensation—either a cash rebate or credit toward space you buy in the future.

Electronic

The stations in your buy should each send you an affidavit of performance. This notarized statement says that your commercials were presented as ordered. Check the affidavit against the buy you contracted for to be sure it agrees with all flights and exact airtimes. Compare the original ratings expectations, too, against any new ratings reports that have arrived. If you find discrepancies, get in touch with the salesperson or rep immediately to negotiate make goods or credits. Timing is important, as you want invoices to reflect any adjustments. Stations will be more cooperative if you complain before the billing is processed.

Out-of-Home

Earlier, you made a preride. Now make a **postride.** Once your showing has begun, drive around to check on the posting. And continue checking regularly during your schedule. Watch for storm damage, street closings that reduce traffic, or the arrival of your competitors on nearby boards or bulletins (thanks to a competing OOH plant that you didn't buy). If they are too near, you can ask your plant for a different location immediately. If you find damage or reduced traffic, negotiate for credit or for additional postings as make goods.

Yellow Pages

Here, your stewardship must be exercised before publication, for once the book is out, it is out for one full year. Check proofs with extreme care. Review headings to make sure you have not missed any that should include your ad or listing. Sign off on final proofs and headings lists, then relax.

How About a Media Service?

Rather than handling the complexities of media planning and buying yourself, you may want to consider working with an independent media service. Most such services are staffed by people who have extensive experience in the media departments of advertising agencies. They are experts in negotiation, squeezing the maximum reach and frequency out of every advertising dollar. They can be helpful in developing your overall strategic planning as well as the media plan and placement.

Media services work for fees and commissions. Many of them got their starts—some years ago when the 15 percent agency commission was still solidly in place—by working for commissions of 10 percent or less. Today, you will probably pay varied fees or commissions. You'll pay more, for instance, for spot television and cable planning and buying than for print, because television and cable take so much more time and effort.

If you deal with a media service, look it over carefully. What you do not want is a service that views media as a commodity—something to buy blindly and thoughtlessly by the pound. What you do want is a service that thinks of media as a creative challenge. Your media service people should believe that the way media is used can make or break your advertising program. They should be constantly on the lookout for new media opportunities—spot availabilities in one-shot or unusual programs that will get high ratings, new publications and revitalized older ones with new formats and fresh young talent attracting upscale readers. Tell your service that where ideas are is where you want to be.

Co-op Advertising: The Manufacturer Pays

If you are a retailer, check on the cooperative advertising support—or ad allowances—available to you from the manufacturers you buy from. In co-op ads, you put the manufacturer's name and logotype in your advertising. Or you "cut in" at the end of the manufacturer's commercial with a local tag line that says the product is available at your store.

Co-op is in every kind of business. There is scarcely any retailer who cannot benefit from it. Co-op dollars go into newspapers, magazines, television and radio, and direct-mail advertising. It is a valuable tool in marketing and promotion.

Benefits to the Maker

The goal of every manufacturer is to get the company product into your store. Your goal is to get it out again, into the hands of customers. Co-op advertising increases sell-in, and it increases sell-through, moving products off the shelf. It does something the manufacturer's national advertising cannot do: It tells the customer exactly where to go to get the product, and it backs up the message with a reason for buying the product today.

How It Works

Your manufacturer sets aside a percentage of the money you pay for purchases; you may use this money at any time within a certain period. Or you may develop a promotion, such as an advertising supplement, and give your suppliers the opportunity to pay for space in it—but promise them exclusives, so they won't find that you have put their competitors in the same promotion. Altogether, through various types of co-op plans, you may be reimbursed from 50 to 100 percent of the costs of your co-op ads.

Tip: If the manufacturer insists on providing its artwork and even its layout exclusively, and your only identification is your name and store logo at the bottom of the ad, think twice. Such an ad probably will not fit in with the look or image you have been working so hard to establish for your store. Customers may not even recognize it as your ad. And don't let a large ad allowance talk you into trying to promote and sell an item that isn't right for your store.

Summary

Media planning and buying is both an art and a science. You start the planning by determining who is your target audience, when you want to reach them, and where to advertise in order to reach them. Unless your budget is unlimited, it is important to decide whether you want to reach more people less frequently or fewer people more frequently. That decision is based on competitive activity, the complexity of your message, how often people buy your product or service, and the extent of promotions you are planning.

Planning calls for a thorough review of the media vehicles that are available to you. For the print media, look at editorial content, publishing schedule, paid or controlled circulation (which is the basis for rates for advertising space), availability of regional advertising space, sizes of space units, and placement or positioning of ads on pages and in feature sections. Also be aware of closing dates for insertion orders and materials, data on pass-along readers as well as subscribers, and cost-per-thousand (CPM).

To get information, talk with salespeople and read rate cards carefully, check out the publication in *Standard Rate & Data Service* (SRDS), and check audits of circulation provided by the Audit Bureau of Circulations (ABC) and the Business Publications Audit of Circulation (BPA).

In reviewing the television and radio media vehicles, you will want to find out about programming and the audiences various programs appeal to, including which dayparts they appear in and the program ratings they achieve (that is, how many households or people who own the equipment to receive a program are actually tuned in). Think about the lengths of commercials needed to tell your story and whether your spots will be more effective if scheduled horizontally (same time and same program on different days) or vertically (various programs all through one or more days). Think about flights of commercials—on for a period, off for an equal period, on again before viewers and listeners quite realize you were off. Think about reach versus frequency in whatever combination gains you high GRPs (gross rating points). Understand that rate cards are highly negotiable, with prices high in a tight market. Be aware of due dates and delivery dates for materials and consider how you will want errors (they do happen, sooner or later) handled—by make goods or invoice credits?

To get information on television and radio media, talk with salespeople. Study rate cards. Check the Nielsen and Arbitron rating services.

In planning for out-of-home (OOH) media, check on locations of vehicles and markets covered. The media buy for poster boards and painted bulletins (signs) is "GRP showings"—packages of boards or bulletins that gain you a given number of gross rating points. Most units can be bought for 30-day periods. Standard sizes are 30-sheets (the typical good old billboard), 8-sheets (the 5-foot-by-11-foot posters outside stores), and large painted bulletins that can be as big as 20 feet high by 80 feet wide.

To get details on out-of-home, talk to salespeople from OOH plants (the firms that own the vehicles and service them) and study their rate cards. Check *The Buyer's Guide to Outdoor Advertising.*

Yellow Pages advertising gives you broad coverage segmented by geographic markets to back up your other advertising. Your ads may run under a number of directory headings, in sizes from a full page down to a couple of boldface lines. Since the publishing schedule is once a year, the closing date may be next week or 12 months away.

To get information, contact your local telephone company's affiliated directory publisher. If you also want to run ads in regional books, the Yellow Pages Publishers Association (YPPA) can put you in touch with an Authorized Selling Representative (ASR) who is in touch with 6,000 directories.

Media buying is a process that begins with a verbal order, whether for print, television, radio, out-of-home, or Yellow Pages. Following initial discussions, an insertion order is placed for print media. The verbal phase in the electronic media involves asking stations for a list of available spots ("avails"), carefully evaluating them, and negotiating over many details, (such as reach that each gets, packaged groups of spots, scheduling of flights for greatest reach and frequency and ultimate GRPs).

Ordering the out-of-home buy begins with taking a preride to view locations of proposed poster boards and bulletins and evaluate them. Negotiation may gain you some bonus postings.

Ordering Yellow Pages ads is a straightforward matter. You fill out a worksheet that functions like an insertion order for newspapers or magazines.

Your planned scheduling must be sure to include enough time for trafficking materials to the media. Newspaper ads and spots for radio and television can be delivered on a short lead time (a couple of days, except for Sunday editions, supplements, and inserts). Magazines may want materials as much as 90 days ahead. Production delivery for OOH varies depending on your buy.

Don't forget to plan on stewardship. Check tear sheets from publications and affidavits from television and radio. Take postrides to look at OOH. Watch for errors and report discrepancies immediately to get make goods or credits. "Never assume nuthin'."

You may want to consider having all this detail handled by a media service. While you will probably get expert negotiators, make sure the service is not one that views media as a commodity to be bought willy-nilly at the lowest price. Look for media minds that understand how to think creatively about media, exploring new ideas and invigorating your entire advertising program.

If you are a retailer, take advantage of co-operative advertising or ad allowances programs offered by manufacturers you buy from. Co-op advertising increases a manufacturer's sell-in to you, and it increases your sell-through to the consumer. But be careful not to fall for control by the manufacturer that overrides or works counter to your own effort to create distinctive advertising that helps to enhance the image of your store.

PART FOUR

HOW ELSE CAN YOU REACH YOUR TARGET? INTEGRATED MARKETING COMMUNICATIONS

The reason integrated marketing is important is consumers integrate your messages whether you like it or not. All marketing is integrated in the mind of the consumer. Your only choice is how that message is integrated.

— Larry Light
president, Arcature Corp.,
a marketing consultancy

Is it advertising or is it promotion? That age-old question is fast becoming irrelevant as a concept called integrated marketing communications, or IMC, gains strength throughout the industry. Experts predict that by the early 2000s, the lines between advertising, direct response, sales promotion, and public relations will have entirely blurred. A budget will be a total marketing communications budget, not an advertising or media or public relations or promotion budget.

IMC is not only a concept. It is also a process. According to Tom Duncan, director of the IMC Graduate Program at the University of Colorado, Boulder, the concept is synergy—a whole that is greater than the sum of its parts. The process is both short-term and long-term. Short-term, the goal is selling, defined as "the strategic development of all messages and media used by an organization to influence its perceived brand value and achieve its marketing objectives." Long-term, the goal of the IMC process is to build relationships, defined as "the process of strategically developing and controlling or influencing all messages which customers and other stakeholders use in forming an image of, and maintaining a relationship with, an organization."[1]

When you get into integrating your marketing communications, you find that *planning* is the most important word in your vocabulary. Planning is more important than execution. In a sense, *what* you plan to do—and then *do*—is more important than *how* you do it. Andy Cochran, who owns a pottery business in New Hampshire, found that out. After trying to launch pottery businesses and having to close them down three times in six years, he realized he didn't know what customers to target or what to sell them. Then he did some market research and found a niche—people who decorate with Early American accessories and want good but reasonably priced reproductions. With $10,000 he started his fourth business, using a carefully planned mix of publicity, advertising, and promotions. He thoughtfully organized schedules of radio commercials and newspaper ads. He preprinted colorful inserts featuring gift ideas and recipes. He mailed postcards regularly to tell preferred customers about special deals. Within 10 years, in 1994, he was looking at annual sales totaling $1.5 million in 6,000 stores across the United States and $1 million in his New Hampshire factory outlet. Probably no one said, "Hey, that's integrated marketing communications!" to Andy Cochran. But that is what it was.

A marketing communications program that is truly integrated includes advertising in any of the media we've discussed so far—media that you pay to transmit your message to its audience. Now let's look at the elements of integrated marketing communications in which you yourself transmit your message or in which your message may be transmitted *gratis*—without payment. They are three:

- *Direct response advertising* is any advertising with which you try to elicit a direct response to you from the reader, viewer, or listener through some kind of response device.
- *Sales promotion* is any activity—except activities in the paid media—that stimulates buying by the consumer during a limited period. It should also inspire more-than-usual support from your sales

1. Duncan, Tom. "Integrated marketing? It's synergy." *Advertising Age*, March 8, 1993, 22. Reprinted by permission.

force and your wholesalers.

- *Public relations* (PR) is often confused with publicity, which is only one element of public relations. Broadly speaking, public relations is a program of action designed to gain the understanding of and acceptance by a wide range of groups of people.

The next three chapters talk about each of these areas.

CHAPTER TEN

Direct Response Advertising

KEY TERMS

bulk mail	*interactive shopping*	*list owner*
catalogue	*Internet*	*lists*
compiled lists	*junk mail*	*merge and purge*
computer networks	*list broker*	*response device*
direct response lists	*list compiler*	*shop-at-home*
house list	*list manager*	*telemarketing*

Direct response includes three basic "media"—the post office, the television tube, and the telephone. To sell directly on each of these and get a successful response, you must know your customer. To know your customer, you need a database. You need information—the more you can get, the better you can fine-tune your direct response advertising program. The key to information is **lists.** Your success with direct response depends on how you select and use lists. If you are inexperienced in this area, you may well consider hiring an expert freelancer to set up your program. But don't turn it over to just any old list service. Check around to see who's good (see Chapter 13).

If you are a retailer, your database may well include not only name, address, and age but such personal information as height, weight, and color of hair and eyes; this information is available in some states from

Department of Motor Vehicles license records and is valuable to you if you are selling such things as apparel or cosmetics. From the same source, you can find out whether your customer owns an expensive car or a cheapie; what color it is; how long ago it was bought; whether it was bought new or used; and whether the family driveway is home to one, two, or more autos or any recreation or off-road vehicles. This is all valuable information if you are selling home furnishings (where it's helpful to have clues about color preference), sports and camping gear, or motor vehicles. On top of all this, you should compile records of past purchases, which you can get by buying lists of manufacturers' warranties on appliances, electronic gear, sports equipment, gardening tools, cameras, all kinds of things. Don't forget lists of magazine subscribers by zip code for the market areas in which you sell, to see what publications your customers like to read.

If you are selling business-to-business, your database can be equally helpful as you input similar information—subscriptions to trade and industrial magazines, patterns of purchase of yours and competitors' products, attendance at conventions and seminars—whatever gives you a profile of your individual prospect or customer.

The point is that the day of the "typical customer" is long past. The more your database tells you about your customer, the better you know him or her. And the better you know where to zero in on his or her life, the more likely you will get a direct response to your advertising. So let your database help you find your customers and tell you who they are and what they like.

Tip: Don't forget the old 20-80 rule: 20 percent of your customers probably account for 80 percent of all your sales. Make sure your database program targets that 20 percent.

When You Make a List

Lists

Your lists are the heart of your direct response program. You use them as the basis for every direct-mail or telemarketing campaign. The information that comes back goes into your database and is added to the lists already there. There are three basic lists to think about:

House list. This is your own list of established customers. It should include everyone who has made a purchase since you started keeping the list, regardless of how much they spent. Depending on what product or service you are selling, your house list may also include for each customer a record of what was bought and what advertising or promotional strategy brought the customer to you; whether he or she bought on credit or paid cash; and any other factors that help to identify the customer geographically, demographically, or psychographically.

You can get valuable information on customers by cross-referencing your house list with a compiled list (see below), such as Department of Motor Vehicles lists or magazine subscription lists.

Direct response lists. These are other peoples' lists. You rent them. Where and how? Through a list broker (see below). The names on these lists are customers of other firms in the direct response business. In other words, they are known direct response buyers. Analyze the lists that are available to you, then rent those that give you names of people who have responded to offers like yours and who are found in similar geographic, demographic, and even psychographic segments of the market. Note: In the business, people say they are "buying" a list when actually they are renting it.

Compiled lists. These are the lists from Departments of Motor Vehicles, manufacturers' warranties, magazine subscriptions, city directories, telephone books that list people by age, occupation, level of education completed, etc. There are a thousand and one sources for these lists.

What kinds of lists work best? Take it from Bob Stone, author of *Successful Direct Marketing Methods,* one of the most complete and authoritative books on the subject:

> In the body of knowledge garnered from hundreds of thousands of list tests, certain findings have emerged. The following statements may be regarded as being reliable *most* of the time:

- A direct response list (with names of those who have shown a propensity to respond by mail) will outpull a compiled list.
- A customer list will outpull outside lists, whether the outside lists are direct response lists or compiled lists.
- People over 35 years old tend, as a group, to respond by mail at a greater rate than people under 35 years old.
- Rural areas tend to respond by mail at a higher rate than urban areas.
- "Hot line" names (those who have responded by mail within the past six months) are likely to be the most productive names available.
- Multiple buyers (those who have purchased two or more times within a season) outpull buyers who have purchased just once within a season.
- The pull from any given list will vary by season, with January being the best pulling month except for offers tied to the Christmas season.
- The pull from any given list will vary by region, state, sectional center, zip code, and census trait.[1]

Brokers, Compilers, and Managers

You cannot get very far in direct response without the help of skilled people known as list brokers, list compilers, and list managers. Here is a brief synopsis of what each one does:

- The **list broker** reviews the profile of your typical customer, gets well acquainted with the product or service you are selling, and then recommends lists that can be expected to produce more customers. The broker is a go-between or consultant who makes the arrangements for you to use another company's lists. The broker does the detail work of placing your order to rent a list, getting clearance from the list owner for your particular use of the list, and following through on delivery to make sure you get the list on time and in the format most useful to you.
- The **list compiler** knows how to pull together lists out of dozens of sources, including those we have already mentioned.

1. Stone, Bob. *Successful Direct Marketing Methods.* 2d ed. Chicago: Crain Books, 1979, 80–81. Reproduced by permission of the publisher.

- The **list manager** is responsible for the maintenance and use of one or more specific lists. Maintenance includes cleaning a list regularly to remove inactive names, correct changes of address, and eliminate duplication (**merge and purge**).

If you keep a house list, you are a **list owner**. As your list builds, you may want to consider renting your list to other advertisers who don't compete with you. For many a list owner, the profits from renting the list are what keep the whole direct response program out of the red. It is worth discussing with a good list broker.

If you are serious about list handling or any other aspect of direct response marketing, a membership in the Direct Marketing Association (DMA) can be quite helpful:

Direct Marketing Association (DMA)
11 West 42 Street
New York, NY 10036
(212) 768-7277

The DMA has a wide membership, including many small businesses.

Is the Post Office Your Medium?

Direct mail is the long-standing keystone of direct response advertising. It represents more than one-third of all the business the U.S. Postal Service does. You can use direct mail in countless ways, sending anything from a straightforward, simple letter in a #10 envelope to such a complicated mailing piece like a 9-inch-by-12-inch four-color envelope containing a several-page letter, a large folded four-color circular, any number of small single note pages, an order form or reply card, and a return envelope (the **response device**).

"Junk Mail"

The majority of direct-mail advertising moves as third-class mail, known as **bulk mail.** It takes longer to reach its destination than first class, but it is considerably less expensive. To use it, you have to obtain a bulk-mail permit with your own permit number, and you have to stick to such rules as sending a minimum number of identical pieces and presorting by zip code—in essence, you do some of the post office's work. Your local post office can give you up-to-date information on current regulations and costs.

A word about so-called **junk mail**. When it comes folded in your newspaper, it is what the newspapers call a freestanding insert—often as many as half a dozen FSIs in one issue. When a similar piece comes in your mail, the newspapers call it junk. They started the bad-mouthing quite a few years ago, and the television and radio people picked up the phrase. It was, of course, simply a way to put down the competition.

The fact is that direct mail works. Many, many people like it—or it wouldn't work. It enables people—precisely the people in your target audience—to shop at home any hour of any day of the week. It is a perfectly respectable means of selling, and its effectiveness is second only to the live one-on-one sales call.

When you set out to produce a direct-mail piece, it is time once again to call on creative talents in copy and art. This is a highly specialized medium. Expert direct-mail copywriters have spent years testing a wide variety of techniques. You want good direct response writers, because the copywriter is doing the selling for you. Your prospect isn't going to meet any other salesperson. Your copywriter is the first, last, and only contact the customer has with you.

Direct-mail copywriters know how to write lead sentences that pull the reader in as relentlessly as the Niagara River whirlpool. They know that people *like* long letters—so long as the reading is interesting right to the end. They have learned how to hold the reader's attention not only with words but with graphics—underlines, indented paragraphs, CAPITAL LETTERS, second colors, and postscripts. (*Note:* Never send off a direct-mail letter without a P.S. that lists one of your most important points. It will get read even if nothing else gets read, because the reader cannot resist looking to see who signed the letter. And in looking for the signature, the reader sees the P.S. and reads it.) Copywriters and art directors are expert, too, in devising ways to put the promise, or benefit, on the outside of the envelope and on every piece inside. Some are sticklers for making sure the offer, its price, and where to send for it appear on each separate piece of paper inside, in case whoever opens the mail lets the pieces scatter.

A good art director knows which typefaces talk right off the page. He or she has a keen, up-to-the-minute feel for colors that are smart and stylish but that are not too far out. And he or she knows that artwork that is mouth-watering or richly textured or gleaming makes the direct-mail piece, and the item you are selling, irresistible.

Catalogues

You don't have to be L.L. Bean or Lands' End or J.C. Penney. Many a small business distributes a **catalogue** to its house list, then expands the target by renting lists. If you sell an inventory of items in any specialty from hobbies and crafts to sports and recreation, from office supplies to computer software, you may find a catalogue quite useful as a direct response device. Catalogues are a growth industry, with continuing annual growth of nearly 6.6 percent and with sales moving up from $51.5 billion in 1992 to some $54.7 billion in 1993, and sales are expected to reach $66.4 billion by 1996. More than half of the U.S. adult population orders merchandise by phone or mail from catalogues each year. The U.S. Postal Service, in a Household Diary Survey in 1991, learned that catalogues received in the mail were opened, looked at, and read or set aside to be read later by 88 percent of Americans.

The key thing to know is that when people open catalogues, they look before they read. Top-notch design is vital. You must have eye-catching graphics, whether you are using simple black-and-white line art (drawings) or full-color photography. Copywriting for catalogues is the art of brevity. You want it short, punchy, descriptive, but with full details on color, size, taste or flavor, and price.

Why Not Just Pick Up the Phone? Telemarketing

Be sure you understand the term. **Telemarketing,** in the vernacular of the business, is *not* shop-at-home via television. (Even *The New York Times* has made the mistake of using the word *telemarketing* in the headline of a story on shop-at-home.) Telemarketing is selling by telephone. By some accounts, this medium gets more direct-marketing dollars than any other.

The only wonder about telemarketing is that it did not start long before it did, for the vast telephone network that connects every American household or business with every other has been established for decades. The technology, such as Wide Area Telephone Service (WATS), was ready and waiting when the marketing experts decided to exploit it. The system consists of two sides: (1) Outgoing calls that solicit business on WATS lines, and (2) incoming calls that make inquiries or place orders on 800 numbers (known as "incoming WATS").

The personal sales call is expensive. The telephone sales call, if handled by an expert, is almost as good, yet costs maybe one-twentieth as much. It can describe and persuade powerfully. It gets excellent results.

But telemarketing can be an annoyance to your customers. Nobody wants to get up from the dinner table to answer the phone and find a salesperson launching into a pitch. One survey found that 27 percent of its respondents considered telephone selling an invasion of privacy, while only 9 percent said the same about direct-mail offers.

Your best bet, if you want to try telemarketing, is to put a service company to work. Its staff people are experts in the art of selling by phone. And, if you are also running direct response commercials on radio or television, the service company can handle the flood of calls that can come in on your 800 number. Look for such companies in your Yellow Pages under the heading "Telemarketing Research & Selling Services." If you want to learn more about the techniques of telemarketing, ask your telephone company about its telemarketing consulting and sales-training programs and workshops.

Tip: Not every product or service can be sold successfully by telemarketing. If yours needs to be demonstrated or explained in great detail, it may be a tough sell on the phone. Be sure the people doing the selling are well trained on the primary benefit you promise so that they can interest the prospect immediately and keep his or her attention. If the entire call is likely to last more than four or five minutes, don't bother. You need another medium.

Can You Sell on the Tube? Shop-at-Home versus Direct Response

You may be wondering if you should be buying television time to sell your products using direct response techniques. Think of television as offering three possibilities:

Direct Response Television

This is the simplest. You ask for the order at the end of your commercial, giving the viewer or listener an 800 telephone number and a mailing address, with the assurance that credit cards are acceptable. The system is really just another version of direct response mail-order advertising, in which you sell directly to the customer, and the merchandise is delivered by mail, UPS, or delivery service.

Be sure your television commercial is strong on demonstration. Stick to merchandise that is priced from low to moderate. A big-ticket item that requires some thought before purchasing is not likely to sell in this medium. You may, however, pull leads for future sales by offering to send more detailed information.

Shop-at-Home Television

Two major purveyors, QVC and the Home Shopping Network (HSN), dominate this field. Neither functions as a direct response advertising vehicle. Rather, they are distribution vehicles. Why? Because they charge you from 40 to 50 percent of sales. That makes it impossible for a retailer, for instance, to make a profit. The charge is high because they handle everything from taking the order by phone to warehousing, sorting, packing, and shipping. In addition, they keep what they learn about the buyer to themselves, so you have no opportunity to build a relationship with a customer.

If you are a manufacturer, however, and want to distribute your products through a high-powered, fast-growing sales medium, the shop-at-home networks can put you in the living rooms of the cable television audience, which is also fast-growing. You will need to present an information sheet on your product for approval, then a sample to be put through rigorous quality tests. Upon approval, you ship individually packaged and labeled product to the network's warehouse so that it will be ready for immediate delivery to the network's customers. Typical products are in the categories of apparel and accessories, toys, camcorders, power tools, home furnishings, jewelry, and health and beauty aids.

Shop-at-home networks seldom handle anything priced under $15. They target men and women 35 to 54 years old who have an annual household income of at least $40,000 and who are accustomed to buying from catalogues and other direct-response vehicles. To find out more, contact:

QVC Vendor Relations
1365 Enterprise Drive
West Chester, PA 19380
(610) 429-8330
Fax: (610) 430-2356

Home Shopping Network
Purchasing Department
P.O. Box 9090
Clearwater, FL 34618-9090
(813) 573-5982

As cable television proliferates, more contenders are climbing into the shop-at-home ring. Among these are the giant retailers, such as Macy's, J.C. Penney, and Bloomingdale's. Working with the Spiegel catalogue, Time Warner has developed Catalog 1. It plans to sell for a number of national catalogue operators—Eddie Bauer, Williams-Sonoma, Sharper Image, the Bombay Company, for instance—with the participants handling their own orders through the same distribution system they use to handle catalogue orders. The companies will get the customer information—names, addresses, phone numbers, buying history—that QVC and HSN prefer not to pass back to their suppliers.

Interactive Shopping

This technology is evolving rapidly. Experts predict that you will soon find interactive communications vehicles to fit every size of business, from giant to small. Their purpose? To give you direct one-to-one relationships with your customers.

Exactly what is interactive technology? It is a combination of the television set, the telephone and its backup cabling system, and a complex array of advanced circuitry and software—perhaps with your personal computer thrown in—that is instantly responsive.

And what does it do? It allows your merchandise to become the message in the living room. Your customer sits at home and asks to see an item you are selling in as much detail as he or she needs before deciding whether or not to buy. Your customer can ask to see a model wearing a specific dress, jacket, coat, sweater, or pair of shoes; a dining room set for a formal dinner; a trail bike plunging down a ravine pathway; the interior of a car or truck—any item in *action* in any perspective from a wide, full-length shot down to a tight close-up. If the customer decides to buy, the order is placed with the push of a button from the couch potato position, and the buyer's credit card is instantly charged. Or if the customer's personal computer is tied into his or her bank's checking account network, the purchase price is deducted immediately from the account.

The advantages? Time saved. For two-earner families with kids in day care. For moonlighters. For everybody who hates to drive to the shopping center or mall, hunt for a place to park, and haul the purchases back out to the car. For everybody whose attitude toward wasting time has already doomed the giant department stores.

But will your customers buy this way? Catalogues have already answered the question. The tremendous growth of selling by catalogue has proved that people do trust the seller. They know they don't have to be in your store, touching your merchandise, to "see" it. When the interactive communications vehicle lets them examine it from every angle, close up or standing back, looking at it from all sides, front and back, top and bottom—you can sell.

Why Not Show Up on Your Customers' Computers?

As this book went to press, **Internet,** the global web of **computer networks,** already connected some 25 million people. It was opened to commercial traffic, including advertising, in 1991, when the U.S. Government announced that it could no longer finance the network infrastructure. It is a powerful direct response marketing tool, useful for many consumer products and services and even more effective for business-to-business advertisers. Martin Nisenholtz, a senior vice president at Ogilvy & Mather Direct, a subsidiary of a major advertising agency, Ogilvy & Mather Worldwide, has suggested six valuable guidelines for advertising on Internet:

1. *Don't send intrusive messages.* No one should receive a commercial message he or she hasn't either asked to receive or doesn't want to receive. For example, if a user requests information

from companies selling ski equipment, companies within this category should be able to send information. But it should be forbidden to add the user's name to a mailing list to which she or he has not subscribed.

2. *Don't sell consumer data without the express permission of the user.* Unlike some commercial services, like mail-order catalogues, where users generally understand that their names will be sold to other businesses, Internet data should remain the user's private property.

3. *Advertising should appear only in designated news groups and list services.* The most objectionable advertising on the Internet is unrelated commercial postings to news groups and conferences, which are usually cross-posted to hundreds of groups. Those who post off-topic commercial solicitations should be warned once by the news groups or conference administrator, then filtered at the source from further postings.

4. *Conduct promotions and direct selling only under full disclosure.* Marketers should be free to offer promotions on the network. But users should be given an opportunity to review the rules, guidelines, and parameters of an offer before they commit to responding.

5. *Conduct research only with the consumer's informed consent.* Marketers should be able to conduct consumer research so long as respondents are made fully aware of the consequences of answering the research questionnaire.

6. *Never use Internet communications software to conceal functions.* Marketers should never use communications software to surreptitiously gather data from unsuspecting users, such as scanning their hard disks for data without permission.[2]

Internet is not the only computer network. Such on-line computer services as Prodigy, CompuServe, and America Online are commercial operations that accept advertising placements. A typical small-business advertiser is Marcia Layton, whose Rochester, New York, firm creates business plans for other small companies. She draws attention to her service by placing classified ads on CompuServe, which has 1.4 million customers.

Summary

A process known as integrated marketing communications (IMC) pulls together advertising, direct response, sales promotion, and public relations to produce a synergistic effect.

To get into direct response marketing, you must have a sound database at your disposal. Success depends on how you use lists that include a wide variety of data—geographic, demographic, and psychographic—on your customers and prospects. Your own house list is the most important. In addition, you will "buy" other firms' direct response lists as well as compiled lists from even broader bases.

A list broker can provide wide experience as well as handle the myriad details of arranging to use lists. A list compiler can help you pull lists together from dozens of sources. A competent list manager can maintain your list and merge and purge it as needed. As a list owner, you may rent your list to others as a profit center.

2. Copyright © 1994 by The New York Times Company. Reprinted by permission.

Direct mail is the keystone of direct response advertising—despite its misnomer as "junk mail" by its competition. Direct mail works for thousands of advertisers and millions upon millions of customers. For this specialized medium, it is important to use experienced copywriters and art directors who know the techniques well. Catalogue selling (one specific area of direct mail) is a growth opportunity for any small business that sells an inventory of items.

Telemarketing, or selling by telephone, is nearly as effective as an in-person sales call, at a fraction of the cost. While it gets excellent results, more than one-fourth of the public consider it an invasion of privacy.

Shop-at-home and interactive marketing on television are the vanguards of the 21st century. Direct response television simply uses mail orders or call-in orders to 800 numbers. Shop-at-home television on its two major networks is more a distribution system than an advertising system because the entire sale and shipping are handled by the network, giving you no feedback on customers. Interactive is evolving rapidly. It enables the customer to ask to see specific items and product demonstrations on television at home at will and to complete the purchase and payment through back-and-forth interaction with the advertiser—thanks to complex circuitry and software—with the advantages of convenience and time saving. Finally, computer networks, which put millions of personal computers in touch with each other, provide a powerful direct response marketing tool for many products and services for consumer and business-to-business markets.

CHAPTER ELEVEN

Sales Promotion

KEY TERMS

ad mat
cents-off
counter card
coupon
dealer
distributor
envelope stuffer
exhibit
hang tag
incentive
in-store demonstration
point-of-purchase
premium
pull-through
push
sell sheet
spec sheet
sweepstakes
trade show
wholesaler

Sales promotion is a group of marketing materials and activities, aside from advertising in the paid media, that you use to stimulate consumer buying, usually during a limited period. If you handle these items this way—as sales stimulators for a specific, short time—they can add to the perceived value of your product or service. They have three other important goals: First, to help support the work of your sales force. Second, to get distributors or wholesalers to push your product through to the dealer or retailer. And third, to increase support from the retail trade or others who resell your product.

What You Want Sales Promotion to Do

The idea of any sales promotion effort is (1) to get some information out and (2) to make something happen as a result. The question is, whom do you want to get the information to and what do you want to happen as a result? There are four target groups to think about: your salespeople, your distributors, your dealers or retailers, and your customers or prospects (see table on page 162–163).

As you scan the items listed in the table,

consider each target and the action you expect.

Your Salespeople

Many of the items on the list go to your sales staff. Your staff needs price lists and **spec sheets** to work from, along with catalogues and up-to-the-minute sales bulletins that inform them on sales volume and geography, etc. You might supply audiovisuals for them to use on sales calls, as part of a complete selling kit, with **sell sheets** and other support material. Sales meetings should be scheduled on a regular basis, with audiovisuals, such as slides, films, or videocassettes, that inform your salespeople about new or improved products.

Don't forget to work up a sales-incentive program that challenges the competitive soul of each salesperson. And be sure they get a good look at your advertising program—proofs of ads, audiocassettes and videocassettes of commercials—*before* it starts appearing in the media. No worthwhile salesperson likes to be left outside that loop.

The action you expect from all this? Thorough knowledge of your product or service and strong motivation on the part of your salespeople to **push** wholesalers and retailers to stock, promote, and sell your product.

Your Distributors or Wholesalers

These folks and others in the distribution chain like to be included, too. If they are putting your products in a showroom, be sure they get signs and banners and product displays. **Point-of-purchase** material is as important here as in the retail outlet. Catalogues and spec sheets, price lists and sales bulletins, looped slide films and self-repeating videocassettes—whatever communicates your story to the trade and motivates action should be there. Never mail an invoice—to a distributor or dealer—without putting an **envelope stuffer** in with your statement.

The expected result? Distributors should be well motivated to push dealers. Every sales promotion piece and every sales promotion activity that you and your salespeople present to the distributors should be aimed at helping them to see the benefits they will gain by convincing *their* target audience—the business places patronized by your ultimate customers—to push your product.

Your Dealers or Retailers

Point-of-purchase displays, **counter cards,** counter folders, **hang tags,** window displays—whatever works in the store should be on your list. The only limit is your budget. Think about **ad mats**—your logotype and illustrations of your products, in a variety of sizes—for the retailer to use in local advertising. Make truck-panel posters and magnetic-backed signs available. Offer envelope stuffers designed with white space for the dealer's imprint. Again, every piece of sales promotion should stimulate support of your total marketing program, motivating the dealer to push the particular items you are promoting.

You may want to offer some items for sale at cost or provide them as **premiums** rewarding quantity orders. Pamphlets for dealer imprint, lighted signs, mechanical or electronic displays—many sales promotion materials are bought by the retailer. There is an excellent reason for selling them rather than giving them: The retailer is more likely to use what he or she has had to pay for.

Your Customers and Prospects

Coupons, cents-off, buy-one-get-one-free, cash rebates, self-liquidating premiums, tie-ins with other products, free samples, **sweepstakes**—the list of sales promotion items and events designed to move the consumer to action is endless. The resulting action you want? **Pull-through.** Your product moves. The dealer reorders. The distributor reorders.

Balance Sales Promotion Against Advertising

Where do you draw the line? Should you forget about advertising and integrated marketing communications and put all your money into sales promotion, where one deal after another gets people at every level—wholesaler, retailer, customer—to buy? No. Because sales promotion does not build a relationship with your customer. If promotion is your only basis for sales, you are sending the message that your product is just another commodity, and the only reason for buying it is price. And that tells the consumer that you didn't price it fairly in the first place and that it wasn't worth the original price.

The answer is balance. If half your budget, or maybe as much as 60 percent, goes to sales promotion, you can produce action effectively. Smart sales promotion activity can give you new customers and entice lapsed customers to come back. It can help introduce a new product among your existing geographics and demographics or help a current product get going in new territory. It can bolster sales when you realize that a sagging quarter is going to hurt your bottom line. But on a quarter-in, quarter-out basis (let alone year-in, year-out), you cannot build a loyal customer base by continually making deals. Your customers won't trust you, and your competition will climb all over you.

With your balanced plan, however—whether your target is the wholesaler, retailer, or consumer—you put sales promotion to work during a specific time to get the customer to buy, and you put advertising to work reinforcing that purchase decision and building loyalty. Result: The perceived value of your product increases.

How Much Goes Where?

In round numbers and across all businesses, about one-third of sales promotion dollars are spent on meetings and conventions. More than 15 percent pays for direct mail (such as announcements of sweepstakes); 13 percent is chalked up to premiums and **incentives** (for example, *Old Farmer's Almanac* free if you subscribe to *Yankee* magazine by a certain date); 12 percent to point-of-purchase displays and materials; and more than 25 percent to promotional advertising (such as freestanding inserts), trade shows, couponing, contests, price deals, and cash refunds.

Coupons are redeemed in 76 percent of

SALES PROMOTION MATERIALS AND ACTIVITIES

Materials	Target Sales	Distributor	Retailer	Consumer
Sales bulletins and circulars	X	X	X	
Catalogues and specification sheets	X	X	X	
Price lists	X	X	X	
Instruction sheets and manuals	X	X	X	X
Distributor catalogue inserts		X		
Sales letters and mailers		X	X	
Distributor and dealer mailers		X	X	
Envelope stuffers		X	X	X
Counter folders			X	X
House magazines	X	X	X	
Motion pictures	X	X	X	
Slide films	X	X	X	
Point-of-sale displays		X	X	
Signs and banners		X	X	
Window displays			X	
Dealer identification signs			X	
Factory signs	X			
Truck panel signs		X	X	
Premiums, novelties, gifts, and souvenirs	X	X	X	X
Traveling displays		X	X	
Packages and labels		X	X	X
Tags and package enclosures		X	X	
Display cartons		X	X	
Counter, aisle, and wall displays; hangers; and signs		X	X	

Materials	**Target Sales**	**Distributor**	**Retailer**	**Consumer**
Sample cases	x	x	x	
Models and layouts	x	x	x	
Sales manuals	x	x	x	
Advertising reprints	x	x	x	
Advertising and sales portfolios and visualizers	x	x		
Visual aids	x	x	x	
Case histories of product use	x	x	x	x
Dealer merchandising manuals	x	x		
Sales kits	x	x		
Letterheads		x	x	
Billheads and shipping labels		x	x	
Dealer mats			x	
Dealer scripts				x
Activities				
Exhibits and shows	x	x	x	
Demonstrations and sampling		x	x	x
Store demonstrations				x
Sales presentations		x	x	
Sales-training courses	x	x	x	
Sales meetings	x	x		
Contests and other sales incentive programs	x	x	x	
Open houses	x	x		
Sweepstakes				x

Source: Liberatore, James H. "Sales Promotion." ***What Every Account Executive Should Know About Merchandising and Sales Promotion.*** American Association of Advertising Agencies, 1988. Adapted by permission.

American households. Refunds are claimed by 45 percent. About 42 percent enter sweepstakes. One out of five people accept free premiums, while just over 10 percent take advantage of self-liquidating premiums. It's no wonder so many small businesses offer coupons put out by local sales promotion firms, distributed by bulk mail, and handed out from the baskets of Welcome Wagon hostesses. If you have a total target audience of 10,000, for instance, you have a target audience of 7,600 *for coupons*—all other things being equal. How many of those redeem *your* coupon depends on the interest in your product and the strength of your coupon offer. Some testing of various coupons will give you a fix on the strongest offer.

Getting Materials Produced and Activities to Happen

Sales promotion is another area where you probably will not want to hire staff. Its creative and production people live in a specialized world. You can find that world in the Yellow Pages under the "Advertising Specialties" and "Sales Promotion Service" headings. But you want to be sure of whom and what you are getting. These people can come in from their design shops with a zillion ideas, many of which will be tried and true and some of which may be trite and drab. It is up to you to recognize the difference. How do you judge? Start by checking around. Ask other advertisers and people in the businesses related to advertising (see Chapter 13). Invite three or four design shops to make presentations. Insist on case histories. Facts. Numbers. Find out who are the shop's customers who are doing the volume business in coupon redemption. Coupons are a key, remember, because they are by far the most successful promotion activity. If the firm you are considering can't do coupons successfully, chances are it can't do other sales promotion activities very well, either.

Important: Keep integrated marketing communications (IMC) in mind when you talk with sales promotion designers. At your first meeting, review your current advertising. Let them know how concerned you are that all sales promotion material tie in closely with the perceptions of your product or service that you are trying to develop. Ask for examples of how they have handled this question for other clients.

Don't hesitate to ask about specifics. Where does the sales promotion service get its printing done—in-house, down the street, or far away? How does this affect reviews, approvals, and delivery dates? How about copywriters—in-house, moonlighters, between-jobbers, or full-time freelancers? Art directors, too. The more you let the service know how knowledgeable you are, the more attention and care you will get and the better the work will be.

When it comes to sales promotion *activities*—**in-store demonstrations,** sweepstakes, contests for consumers, participation in trade shows and conventions—you want skilled experts who have "been there before." Check your best sources and review several firms before you make a commitment.

Trade shows and **exhibits** are a specialty unto themselves. They give you an excellent opportunity to demonstrate how your product or service works and to introduce new products or product improvements. Potential customers can compare competing products at other booths. You can hand out any kind of sales promotion material you want to—from pamphlets to samples to videotapes, and you don't have to pay for postage! And you can schedule razzle-dazzle entertainment that pulls in a crowd alternately with step-a-little-closer-folks demonstrations that sell hard.

Tip: Two key things to remember about trade shows and exhibits: First, allow plenty of time. A top-notch exhibit cannot be designed and built overnight. Try to start briefing your sales promotion firm's creative people 60 to 90 days before the date of the show. Second, put professionals to work. You want idea people who can create an exhibit that will be remembered long after the show closes. Piling a collapsible table, a couple of uncomfortable folding chairs, a box full of literature, and the wrinkled company banner into a company van and taking off for the convention center, where you have paid good money for a booth, is not the answer.

Who's in Charge?

Coordinating your sales promotion program with your entire integrated marketing communications program is vital. Everything must pull together to give you the synergy that can result in a bottom line you want to sing about. But even today, despite all the experience that many companies have had with IMC, many others still do sales promotion as an afterthought. And many still allow sales promotion to be the sole province of the sales director, a situation that invites cronyism and exclusivity.

If you yourself are handling your company's advertising program, make sure your sales department knows that you are coordinating the sales promotion work. If you are delegating the advertising to someone else, include sales promotion as a respected member of the IMC—and then keep an eye on it, for sales promotion, more than direct response or public relations, has a tendency to want to go its own way.

Summary

The primary job of any sales promotion material or activity is to stimulate buying by the consumer during a limited period. Sales promotion also supports your sales force, encourages wholesalers to push your product, and increases retail support. Its specific purposes are to provide information and induce prompt action.

The targets of sales promotion are your company salespeople, your distributors, your dealers, and your customers. The large variety of sales promotion materials and activities ranges from price lists, spec sheets, and sales meetings for salespeople to signs, audiovisuals, and envelope stuffers for distributors; from point-of-purchase displays and counter folders for retailers to coupons, sweepstakes, and self-liquidating premiums for consumers.

You must be careful to balance sales promotion programs, which are price-oriented, with your advertising program, which is value-oriented. If you make promotion your only basis for sales, you convey the idea that you are selling a commodity on price alone.

One-third of sales promotion dollars are spent on meetings and conventions. Lesser percentages (all less than 15 percent) go to direct response, premiums and incentives, and other miscellany. Some 76 percent of Americans redeem coupons, while 45 percent claim refunds, and 42 percent enter sweepstakes.

Specialists who create and produce sales promotion materials and activities can be found in the Yellow Pages and by networking. Ask them to make presentations on their experience and capabilities and check them out carefully, keeping your integrated marketing communications in mind.

Trade shows and exhibits are a special area that reach retailers and consumers with demonstrations and a chance to compare competitive products. Allow plenty of time for design and construction of your exhibit booth.

Keep a watchful eye on the coordination of sales promotion with advertising in your total program. Don't let sales promotion become an afterthought or the sole province of your sales director, lest you lose the synergy that your integrated marketing communications program is trying to achieve.

CHAPTER TWELVE

Public Relations

KEY TERMS

benchmark
biography
community relations
crisis communications
employee relations
external public relations
fact sheet
feature story
financial relations
internal public relations
media event
media placement
media relations
news story
press conference
press kit
press list
press release
public affairs
publicity
public relations audit
public relations plan
sidebar
situation analysis
special events
spokesperson
third-party endorsement
trade press
query

The public is whoever is out there beyond the door of your own office: your employees, neighbors, customers, prospects, the industry or field of business in which you work, the communications media, the investment and financial community, your government from local to federal, and a bunch of special-interest groups any one of which may be looking closely at you. Whether you like it or not, and whether you think about it or not, the fact is that you have relations with all these people and groups. The practice of public relations is how you deal with them. It is another of the three basic components of integrated marketing communications (IMC).

It's not just **publicity.** Many people have the wrong idea about public relations. They confuse it with publicity, which is simply one aspect of it. Publicity is an important part of the total, for anything that is said or printed about you and your business in either the general press or the trade press is being said by an outside party. That makes it an endorsement that carries an authority far stronger than you get when you place a paid advertisement. And, generally speaking, it is the relationship with the press that demands the majority of the time and attention of any public relations program.

How a Public Relations Program Can Help You

A well-planned, continuing public relations (PR) program can take advantage of any number of opportunities both internally and externally.

Internal Public Relations

The goal of public relations activities within the company is to maintain and boost company morale, helping to make your people proud to work there and to heighten their interest in what the company is doing. **Employee relations** becomes a key part of the total program. It is especially important to gain recognition for your people and their achievements and to keep them informed on company plans, new products, sales successes, management changes, and anything else that makes them feel they are responsible members of the company family.

External Public Relations

Here your public relations program works to increase awareness of your product or service and strengthen the image that your customers and others have of you. It can help you attract new employees, introduce a new or improved product, and maintain or improve relations with your neighbors and surrounding community. It can be invaluable when public issues that may affect your business either favorably or unfavorably come up in city hall, the state capital, or Washington. Special events—a store or factory opening, a sales meeting or convention, an anniversary celebration—provide excellent public relations opportunities. And a well-rounded public relations program can prepare you for the inevitable day when a crisis of one sort or another darkens your sky.

Your Public Relations Plan

How do you get a public relations program under way? You need to take paper and pencil in hand and work out a **public relations plan.** In basic structure it is not all that different from your marketing plan or the advertising plan within it, for it should include a number of similar elements:

1. Situation Analysis

Begin with what you know right now about your public relations situation. Think of this as a **public relations audit.** List everything your organization now does or publishes in communicating with your internal and external audiences. For example:

- Publishes employee newsletters and bulletins
- Sponsors employee events (such as infor-

mational or in-service training lunches, field trips, sports teams, clubs)

- Publicizes any subject from employee promotions to new products to company events (such as a factory dedication, store opening, the installation of new machinery or equipment) and community events (such as lending use of office phones and WATS lines for a local fund-raising telethon, participation in a parade or fair)
- Lobbies for or against government issues involving regulation or taxation related to your business or industry

In developing your audit, look for places in your situation analysis where it will be valuable to establish **benchmarks.** Do you have research now that establishes the extent of awareness of your organization or that analyzes opinion about it in a qualitative sense? It will be important later on, when you want to evaluate the success of your public relations program, to know where you were when you started.

Your public relations audit must be brutally honest. To help make it so, get opinions from all sides about your company's strengths and weaknesses—from employees present and past, from customers present and past, from others in your general field (such as retailers in home furnishing, fast food, hobbies and toys, or whatever; or business-to-business friends, associates, and customers). Check out any stories that have appeared about your company in the **trade press** or general press that you did *not* originate or instigate.

To complete your analysis, be sure to include a summary of changes that may be going on in your particular business environment or in the regional economy that should be listed as problems or opportunities for public relations activities.

2. Public Relations Objectives

Now state your goals. Many of these may seem redundant, as they are also your advertising goals, but they need their own attention as public relations goals. For example, one goal may be to help launch a new product with your salespeople, distributors, retailers, and consumers, but by using public relations to supplement your advertising techniques. Among the objectives you may want to list:

- Establish and promote awareness of your company and its products and services (if your benchmark research tells you that you just aren't well known)
- Change perceptions (if your benchmark discloses an inaccurate impression—for example, "those things aren't built to last" or "that place is a sweatshop")
- Improve the morale of employees (if your benchmark uncovers negative attitudes—indifference to customer relations or a lack of pride in one's work)
- Help bolster a sale or promotion
- Encourage a positive image of the company in the financial community (assuming yours is a public company)

As you work over your public relations plan, you may want to come back to these objectives and prioritize them. Your program may not be able to do everything at once, although it probably can do more than one thing at a time. Working out these elements will help you to see where the priorities lie.

3. Public Relations Targets

Once again, you turn to geographics, demographics, and psychographics. Define the audiences you want to reach—by age, sex, occupation, education level, household income, zip code, family size, and whatever more specific data helps to pinpoint the identity of a particular public.

4. Public Relations Strategies

These are your basic plans-within-the-plan for achieving your objectives. You may want to list a number of strategies. Put them in order of priority. The three that are most likely to come first are media relations, employee relations, and special events. Because these three are so important, they are described later in this section. Other strategies worth thinking about:

Community relations. Among the tactics that carry out this strategy are sponsorship of Little League or Pop Warner teams (your name appears on the uniforms and in the sports news), funding the planting of flower beds on your city's traffic islands or at busy street corners (your name appears on the sign among the petunias), participation in fund-raising for tax-exempt 501(c)3 organizations (you or your CEO appears in the kickoff photo or speaks at the concluding banquet), sending speakers from your firm to address the luncheons and dinners of local woman's clubs, Rotary, Kiwanis, Lions, and other service clubs.

Trade and industry relations. Tactics here may include serving on committees to review and advise on environmental concerns, zoning regulations, crime prevention, quality control, or any number of such issues. You and your company stand to gain significant exposure when such activities work through to positive results.

Minority and intercultural relations. Your company's involvement, through you, your CEO, or your human resources manager, may produce meaningful results from a public relations as well as human-relations standpoint.

Public affairs and government affairs. Tactics under this strategy include two kinds: (1) serving on committees responsible for developing effective public policy and (2) lobbying legislators and regulatory agents on pending legislation or regulation. This is a risk area, as every issue of this type has a winning side and a losing side. But if you wind up on the losing side, it is better than not being on any side at all, for the last public relations result you want is to have people perceive you as an expert at waffling.

Financial relations. If stock in your company is available to the public, you must include a strategy for creating and maintaining the confidence of investors. Tactics range from production of a comprehensive annual report to regularly scheduled newsletters addressed to the financial community.

5. Public Relations Budget

Public relations is different from advertising, for you cannot buy space or time for it in the media. Nor can you budget dollars for "buying" your community's interest in and understanding of your organization, or for other strategies discussed above. But you must plan to pay for two things: time and expenses.

The time you pay for may be that of a staff person, a freelance public relations expert, or a public relations agency (see section Who Does It? later in this chapter). The expenses are for research, printing, travel, postage, production of audiocassette and videocassette news releases, and such—all the things usually described as "out of pocket." When you get your public relations plan down to a working model you can guesstimate these with reasonable accuracy.

6. Public Relations Evaluation

Your plan should include some means of gauging the results of your program. To evaluate results, you have to establish a position from which you started—the benchmark, mentioned earlier. Actually, you will need benchmarks for each of the strategic areas.

Many of the established market research techniques, for both pretesting and posttesting, are applicable for evaluating your public relations effort, such as:

- Focus-group interviews, in which an experienced interviewer probes the opinions of several people in a small group
- Public opinion surveys, which ask people on the street or in malls or shopping centers how they feel about your company, product, or service, and why
- Motivational research, which digs into psychological reasons for judgments, behavior, and attitude—why folks like, hate, or don't care about your company
- Effectiveness research, which measures the effect of your public relations program on the target audience
- Content analysis, which analyzes press clippings and television and radio recordings to see what the media are saying about you and how they present the information—in talk shows, as hard news reports, as soft news in features or discussion programs

Make sure the evaluation section of your plan is clear about press clippings and television and radio transcripts and recordings. These are nice to have, and you can count them and put them in piles and in scrapbooks. But they don't tell you anything about how the reader or listener or viewer received them or reacted to them. Some people say, "Wow! Think how much all this might have cost if we'd been buying the same amount of advertising time and space!" Wow, yes. But if you had been buying it, you would have wanted to have some way of measuring its effectiveness.

Three Key Strategies

Media Relations

Your public relations person will probably find that the majority of the time on the job is spent dealing with the press. "Be prepared" and "be frank and truthful" are the two best bits of advice you can give him or her. Take it from Jack O'Dwyer, a longtime public relations reporter who publishes the major directory of public relations firms, on the importance of "openness":

> Remember that analysts and reporters are writing stories that must have a plot.

Plots demand counterplots or the story will be boring. Obstacles overcome, fierce competition, failures along the way, and mistakes made are all necessary ingredients of good stories.

When you deal with a reporter or analyst, you have an expert audience that is paying complete attention to every word that you are saying. You have to have a full and interesting message—not just an advertisement.[1]

Your tactics in following through on your media relations strategy should include two types of stories that reporters and editors are always looking for: news stories and feature stories.

If you have a **news story** to offer, you write up a **press release**. Begin by asking yourself, What is the news? News is something that nobody knew before. It may be that something happened—you have hired someone important, produced something unusual, installed a remarkable piece of equipment, introduced a new line. It may be that something is going to happen—you are announcing the news in advance. You must learn to recognize a good news story, and you must be sure that the lead sentence of the press release tells the reader what the news is, in plain English.

Next, ask yourself another question: Where do we send this? You—or your public relations person—must know who is looking for what kind of news. The list of publications for news within your trade or industry may be obvious. But you may have news that will interest any of a host of editors—those responsible for news of business, real estate, fashions, food, sports, entertainment, and so on in local, regional, and perhaps national newspapers and magazines. And don't forget television and radio, which consume enormous amounts of news, mostly in very small bites. So your media relations strategy must include knowing the potential news outlets and their editors.

The **feature story** is different. If you think you have a story to tell that is not news but that can be interesting to readers (or listeners or viewers), you do not write a press release. You write a **query.** This is a short (ideally, one-page) description of what the feature will be about and why it will be interesting to the medium's audience. Here it is important to lead with the "hook" or "angle" that will intrigue the reader: "When 18-year-old Bertha T. went to work at the XYZ Company in 1945, she had no idea that in 1995 she would..." Or "Fred M.'s 33-year-old pruning shears suddenly wouldn't cut. He examined the tool. The little brass edge where the blade struck was gone. Lost in the underbrush. He saw the fine print stamped on the handle: Seymour Smith & Son Oakville, Conn. USA. Was the company still there?"

Again, where to send it? You compile a list of likely publications for a story on a longtime employee or on a free-replacement-of-parts policy that has continued for decades. This list is the first of many items you will find useful in carrying on a public relations program. Things to have:

- *Press list.* A **press list** includes every newspaper, magazine, television or radio station, with the name of the person to contact, that may be considered a likely **media placement**—even those that have never published or broadcast a word

1. O'Dwyer, Jack. "How to Hire and Get the Most from Outside PR Counsel." *O'Dwyer's Directory of Public Relations Firms:* 1993. Reprinted by permission.

about your company but, conceivably, might some day. Make it practical. List name of contact (reporter, editor), full address, and phone number for each. Organize by media categories and alphabetize by name of publication or station. Review the press list before sending out each release or query and send only where you have a reasonable expectation of placing the story. Clean your list at least once a year—people change jobs and news assignments.

- *Backgrounders.* Prepare fact sheets on your company, products, store, or featured merchandise. Write up short biographies of key people whom reporters or feature writers may want to contact.
- *Press kits.* Assemble standby **press kits** that include **fact sheets, biographies,** and photographs of your key people as well as of your products, store, or plant. Action photos of people at work, with interesting captions describing the scene, are more likely to be picked up and used by the press than beauty shots of a piece of equipment or a well-lighted interior. Send or hand out the press kit to any reporter or feature writer who is interested. When you have a major item of news, include the kit along with your press release.
- *Media events.* Never call a **press conference** unless you absolutely have to. It puts a big demand on press people, who must travel to the site, sit through the conference, then get back to their desks, when they never have enough time in a day as it is. Most of the time they could have gotten the story from your press release, press kit, and a few follow-up phone calls.

But you may have occasions when only a press conference will do—such as during a crisis (see below) or when you need to make a major announcement at which you want to demonstrate a product or service or present prominent citizens (business and community leaders, for example) who will have something worthwhile to say to the news people. Give at least 48 hours notice in a brief invitation that lists date, time, place, subject (described in a sentence or two), and participants. Serve Danish pastries and coffee. The press is always hungry.

Another **media event** is the tour. Once in a great while you may want to invite the media to come around not with a deadline story in mind but in anticipation of news to come. If you are getting a new store or factory ready to open, for instance, you can give them an insider's look *before* the grand opening to which you will invite the public. This gives them time to investigate, send in their own photographers, and work up features and **sidebars** (specific short pieces on a special person or aspect connected with the main story).

Tips: Two temptations to resist: First, don't hound a reporter about your story. If it hasn't appeared by the time you think it should have, there may be any number of reasons why. More important stories may have pushed it aside temporarily (or even permanently). An editor may have asked for a rewrite. Someone involved in the process may be out sick, slowing things down. You never know. Second, don't try to control your story. Reporters and editors have their points of view. Publicity is not advertising. You are not paying the media to run your story, and you have no control over what happens to it. You are *not* entitled to see it before it appears in print.

Employee Relations

This second major strategy of public relations deals with your inside audience. Its purpose is to create or improve the communications between management and employees as well as among employees. The ultimate goal is to boost employee morale so productivity increases. The tactical elements that carry out this strategy may include the following:

- *Surveys and audits.* You need to decide what kind of information should be conveyed to whom. What do your employees know now and what should they know about the company? Are they as well informed as they should be about its history, products, and successes? What can they learn from its failures? What current problems should they be told about, so they can help solve them? What will focus-group interviews among employees—conducted by fellow employees in whom they have confidence—reveal?
- *Plan.* Based on what you find out from the research, develop a plan on paper for both written and verbal communication. This may include a wide variety of items, such as newsletters, notices for bulletin boards, handbooks, audiovisual presentations at meetings. Don't forget the families of employees. A newsletter produced specifically for the folks at home can be a powerful morale booster.
- *Production.* Material must be researched and written, designed, printed, and distributed. Your public relations director or coordinator may uncover an in-house computer whiz who can turn out fine desktop publishing efforts. For many items, you don't need to go on press. A good copying machine can provide the print run you need for a small business.

The important thing about employee relations as a strategy in your total public relations program is to get it going and keep it going. Don't miss publication dates. Find ways to be responsive to feedback from employees, whether it is positive or negative. Encourage volunteers. Look for talent that hasn't been discovered. If you have union contracts, be sure to include shop stewards in the planning as well as execution stages. Don't let people feel they have been left out of a loop they should be in.

Special Events

You have only three limits on this third public relations strategy: time, talent, and budget. Putting on special events takes all three. What are public relations special events? Anything that brings people together in some relationship to your business. They may be for employees only or customers only or open to the public. Think of open houses, plant dedications, store openings or expansions, parades, seminars, customer tutorials (on fashions, makeup, food, gardening, decorating, photography, travel, videotaping, whatever relates to your business), anniversaries, holidays. To fulfill your special-events strategy, a number of tactics may be useful:

- *Set objectives.* Figure out what it is you want to do or have happen. It can be as simple as: Get people to come to the store in the evening. An event that is publicized well can bring them in.

- *Decide what kind of event to have.* The event dictates a number of related elements: whom to invite, what refreshments to serve, what support materials will be needed (notebooks, name tags, audiovisual projection equipment, etc.).
- *Project a time line.* On a spread sheet, note deadlines for start and completion of each logistical step.
- *Create written materials.* Invitations, programs, complimentary tickets or passes (if attendance is limited) must be written, printed, and distributed.
- *Take care of administrative details.* Coordinate mailings, personal phoning to VIPs, briefing of speakers.
- *Tie in to media relations.* Make sure the press knows no later than anyone else and preferably sooner. Plan for a press table or press section of the room or hall.
- *Brief your own people.* Don't leave your employees in the dark. Tie in to employee relations via their newsletters, bulletin boards, and meetings.
- *Evaluate.* Make sure your plan includes some means of analyzing the event afterward—its results, good or bad. Include evaluation questionnaires in materials for participants. Keep records. Put the experience to work next time.

Special Strategy: Crisis Communications

One strategy that you hope you never have to use is **crisis communications**. But it is better to have thought about what you will do in a crisis and to have made a plan than to be caught unprepared when bad luck strikes. The press arrives in a hurry to report on bad news, and it won't wait for you. Journalists want someone to talk with and question, and if you are not ready with that someone, they will find someone who is ready to talk. As you know from watching television news, there are always people ready to talk, even if they don't know what they are talking about.

Put a plan together. Update it whenever conditions change—certainly you should review it at least once a year. Think what if: What if we had a fire and had to close the place down? What if an accident in the plant seriously injured or killed someone? What if we lost business and had to cut back a significant percentage of employees? What if we had a strike and couldn't meet customers' orders? What if an employee were charged with embezzlement, sexual harassment, or white-collar crime? You can imagine dozens more what if's.

Among the tactics you should line up to carry out your crisis strategy are these:

- *Confidential information.* Keep your public relations director or coordinator well informed whenever a crisis is impending. Don't wait until something happens to start getting a response ready.
- *Think about possible responses.* Evaluate their implications. Look for positives, even in the worst scenarios, and try to plan ways to draw attention to these.
- *Tell your people.* When bad news hits, level with your employees, so they won't start or fuel rumors. Have a system in

place that can communicate with them immediately, without waiting for the routine newsletters or bulletins.

- *Designate the spokesperson.* Know ahead of time whose job it is to stand up and answer questions from the press. Make it someone who is articulate and confident (but not conceited or arrogant) and who understands the importance of being truthful and straightforward with the press. Make sure that all inquiries from the news media go to this person. In any kind of major crisis, the CEO should be the **spokesperson** for the company. Why? Because the responsibility comes with being the CEO and because good reporters will push through to where the buck stops.
- *Anticipate the tough questions.* Have an answer ready for the very first question that every astute reporter will ask: When did you first become aware of this problem and what did you do about it then?

Who Does It

You can choose any of three ways to carry out your public relations plan. One way is to assign the entire responsibility to a member of your staff—probably as an added chore on a part-time basis. Unless you have someone who is one humdinger of a writer and organized right down to his or her toenails, you are likely to be disappointed. Public relations is not something to learn on the job, part-time, in a small business. But you can delegate the coordination of the program to a staff person. Or you may want to handle it yourself. If you are the CEO or president, you will be wise to keep quite close to the public relations program—far more close, for instance, than you need be to your advertising program. Public relations is CEO work.

Your second option is the freelancer. See Chapter 4 for a discussion of freelance types—moonlighters, those between jobs, early retirees, and full-time freelancers—but do not simply hire an advertising copywriter. When you are considering any one of these, make sure he or she is experienced in public relations. Few copywriters from advertising are able to turn around and exercise public relations skills (and vice versa). You want someone who has top-notch writing skills, who understands business, and who can talk convincingly on the phone without being a BS artist. (Theoretically, the BS went out of public relations nearly 100 years ago, when public relations pioneer Ivy Lee declared the end of press agentry by announcing a "Declaration of Principles," but not everyone has heard about it yet.)

Maybe You Should Hire a Public Relations Firm

The third way to handle your public relations program is to turn it over to a public relations firm. Such firms are everywhere. Under "Public Relations Counselors" you will find two or three firms listed in many of the Yellow Pages directories for towns with populations of fewer than 20,000. Cities of 50,000 or so list a dozen or more. Bigger cities have even longer lists. So find-

TEN RULES FOR SHOPPING FOR A PUBLIC RELATIONS FIRM

1. Obtain complete current account lists of prospective firms with names and phone numbers of client contacts.
2. Check with media in your city and industry to find out which PR firms and counselors are highly regarded.
3. Ask that the people who will be serving your business attend the firm's presentation to you.
4. Keep your review committee small.
5. Beware of overpromising by the PR firm. You will be the biggest factor in the success of PR effort.
6. Insist on fast start of service. Test media contacts of firm right away.
7. PR is supposed to be efficient. Beware of high-cost communications materials like booklets, advertising, sales promotion devices. Advertising is often pitched as PR.
8. **Third-party endorsement** is key element of PR. Press, analysts, government reps must fully understand your story, including negative elements.
9. Don't hire a PR firm in the hope of reaching its other clients.
10. Beware of the firm that brags about its famous clients and can "squeeze you in." It may have little time for you.

Source: O'Dwyer, Jack. "How to Hire and Get the Most from Outside PR Counsel." *O'Dwyer's Directory of Public Relations Firms:* 1993. Adapted by permission.

ing public relations firms is easy. Choosing the right one is more complex.

The first thing you should know is that the size of the firm is not important. Good professionals work in public relations firms of all sizes. What is important, when you consider any firm, is who its clients are and what kind of work it does for them. See the box above for Jack O'Dwyer's ten rules on shopping for a public relations firm.

The O'Dwyer Directory is a good place to start your search. It should be in your public library's business reference section, or you can order it directly from the J.R. O'Dwyer Co., Inc., 271 Madison Avenue, New York, NY 10015; phone: (212) 679-2471.

The Directory includes a geographical index, so you can find firms near you, and a special-skills index, so you can find firms that have experience in your category of business. Some of the categories included:

- Agribusiness
- Beauty and Fashion
- Books and Publications
- Educational Institutions
- Entertainment/Theatre
- Financial Public Relations/Investor Relations
- Foods, Beverages
- Foreign Markets
- Health
- High-tech/Industrial
- Home Furnishings
- Minority Markets
- Political Candidates
- Professional Services
- Society
- Sports
- Travel

The book contains listings on more than 2,000 firms, and in 80 percent of the listings, it also includes who the firms' clients are. O'Dwyer advises steering clear of firms that don't list their clients. He notes how one firm for many years made no new-business pitches. Instead, it simply gave prospects a complete list of all its clients, with contact names and phone numbers, and urged the prospect to call them. The firm usually got the business despite full presentations by its competitors.

A valuable section of the directory cross-indexes more than 15,000 clients of public relations firms, so if you know a company name you can look up its public relations firm's listing.

Some of the points made in Chapter 6 on hiring an advertising agency apply equally to your search for the right public relations firm. Invite several firms to come in and talk. See whom you feel comfortable with. You want the chemistry to be right. Look at their clippings. Run through their off-the-air tapes showing how their video news releases were used. Read their employee newsletters and bulletins. Ask about pretesting and posttesting they've done on attitudes and awareness.

And go see *them*. Traipse through their offices. Sniff around. You want to come away sensing that the firm is busy, has the latest copying and faxing and data retrieval technologies, and is a fun place to work in.

Public relations fees. How much should you expect to pay? An individual freelancer may charge you anywhere from $20 to more than $100 per hour. Public relations, incidentally, is a field in which the most common method of payment is by the hour.

A public relations firm is likely to ask for payment in one of three common forms:

- *Retainer fee.* You and the firm agree on a monthly fee, with the public relations firm providing service as you need it. The flat rate is billed in advance, and you pay it regardless of how much or how little the service is used. This system works best if you have some in-house public relations capability or are using a freelancer for the routine work but need counseling on major issues or other special help now and then.
- *Minimum monthly fee.* Here, you agree on a monthly fee based on the number of hours the public relations firm estimates it will spend—usually a minimum guaranteed to the public relations practitioner or firm and a maximum not to be exceeded unless you, the client, approve. You pay this amount each month in

advance. The public relations firm's people log their time and it is charged against the monthly minimum according to each person's hourly rate. (One longtime public relations expert figures that the salary a public relations firm should pay each person who serves you should be from 33 to 50 cents of every dollar you pay the firm.)

- *Project fee.* In this arrangement you pay for projects one at a time. Say you want to put on an event. The public relations firm figures out a price based on time and expenses. Or you want a feature story placed in a trade publication. The firm sets a price for querying editors, writing the feature, and following through.

The monthly fee (either retainer or minimum) for a public relations firm may be anywhere from less than $1,000 to more than $10,000. Freelancers may work for well under $1,000 a month. A firm that is carrying overhead costs on office space, even for as few as three or four people, is not likely to take on a client whose budget is under, say, $10,000 a year. In your chats with firms during your search, ask probing questions about how much attention and exactly what kind of service you can expect at various rates.

Expect to reimburse actual amounts for travel, production, and out-of-pocket expenses (postage, copying, toll phone calls, and the like). If the public relations firm wants to slap a 15 percent markup on these expenses, you want some other public relations firm.

When you talk with a public relations firm about handling your business, make it clear that you want to know about the firm's attitude toward and experience with all the public relations strategies—not just media relations. And when you talk with some of the firm's clients, check out these areas.

When you have selected a public relations firm, it will draw up a letter of agreement that clearly states the payment method and any minimums or maximums to be maintained. The agreement should be cancelable upon 30 days' written notice by either side.

Summary

The practice of public relations is that of dealing with a number of publics, ranging from employees and neighbors to government and special-interest groups. Publicity is but one aspect of the subject, but the relationship with the press often commands the majority of time spent on public relations.

An internal public relations program can help maintain and boost employee morale. An external program works to increase awareness of your company and bolster its image. To handle public relations for both areas, it is important to develop a comprehensive public relations plan. The plan begins with situation analysis, or a public relations audit, so you know where you were when you started. Next, state objectives—such as to promote awareness of or change perceptions of your company or product, improve employee morale, support a sale or promotion, encourage a positive image in the financial community.

The plan covers target audiences and strategies for reaching them, including community, trade, and minority relations. Your budget must cover time charges for public relations services (the majority of the cost) and out-of-pocket expenses (postage, some printing, travel, etc.—the lesser part of the cost). Finally, your public relations plan should include methods of evaluating the results on a regular basis by comparison with the benchmarks established when you started.

Three major strategies are media relations, employee relations, and special events. Media relations is dealings with the print, television, and radio journalists—the press. You get publicity with news stories or feature stories. News stories are usually offered to the press as written press releases ready for publication. Features are offered as queries suggesting articles to be written by the publication or stories to be produced by the television or radio station, or those to be prepared by your public relations person.

Careful maintenance of a press list is important to the media relations operation. Backgrounders, fact sheets, and biographies of your key people should be prepared. Press kits assemble these elements as well as photographs and company literature—if it is pertinent as background material for a journalist. Don't indulge in a press conference unless you have something of considerable substance to impart to the press.

Employee relations is the second major public relations strategy. Its goal is to boost morale—and, consequently, productivity—by improving communications between management and employees as well as among employees. Your plan may include newsletters, audiovisuals, meetings, and events. It is important to keep a program going regularly and to include key people in planning and running it.

The third key strategy, special events, includes any and every kind of event from anniversary celebrations to plant dedications, from customer tutorials to open houses. Only time, talent, and budget limit your opportunities. But handle the myriad logistical details with care and allow plenty of time.

Crisis communications is a special area of public relations that you hope you never need. Nevertheless, you should think about worst-case scenarios and be ready for them, keeping your public relations director informed of any pending crisis, looking for positive responses to have ready, informing employees so they don't start rumors or fuel them, and—most important—designating a single official spokesperson for the company so that the press and all others know whom to talk to. In any serious situation, your CEO should be that spokesperson.

Your public relations people may be on staff, if the work load justifies maintaining a full-time pro. Assigning the task to a part-timer will probably bring you disappointment. A freelancer will probably work out better, but make sure he or she is experienced in public relations. A public relations firm is the other alternative. Good public relations people are found in all firms, large or small.

If you are shopping for a public relations firm, get the names and phone numbers of its current clients and talk with several of them. Check in with media people for their opinion. Use *O'Dwyer's Directory of Public Relations Firms* to find those that have experience in your category of business and to see whom they serve. Invite several firms in. Review their samples. Feel their chemistry. Visit their offices. When you choose one, work out either a retainer fee (flat monthly charge) or a minimum monthly fee or plan for a fee-per-project arrangement. Make sure the firm you hire has a good track record on placing stories with the media (that is, knows how to get publicity) but is also capable in the other public relations strategies. And insist that it get off to a fast start with media placements.

PART FIVE

FOR FURTHER READING AND MORE INFORMATION

CHAPTER THIRTEEN

How Can I Learn More About the Business?

KEY TERMS

ad club	*internship*	*resource center*
association	*job bank*	*schmooze*
award	*networking*	*speakers' bureau*
directory	*newsletter*	*workshop*
	professional development	

Where Can I Schmooze with Advertising People?

Small businesses like to share information. Owners and executives of small businesses count on referrals by word of mouth in many situations. They use **networking** to market products and services. At meetings of any number of business groups, such as Kiwanis, Rotary, Lions, Chamber of Commerce, you can swing the conversation to advertising and pick up information on media, printers, production houses, freelance writers and art directors, public relations people, sales promotion shops—you name it.

Ad Clubs

Associations more specifically related to the business are looking for you. Advertising clubs are active in many American cities. Most of them belong to the national organization, the American Advertising Federation (AAF), which represents nearly 50,000 advertising professionals who belong to some 220 affiliated clubs around the country. AAF is the only national advertising organization that represents all segments of the industry: advertisers, ad agencies, media, and companies that service advertising. The organization runs major **award** competitions nationally and encourages local club competitions.

Its college and university chapters link today's active ad people with academicians and future advertising professionals. An AAF club is sure to be within your driving range if not in your town. Its luncheon or dinner meetings, probably held monthly, can give you excellent **schmoozing** opportunities. If you can't find the club nearest you by asking around, contact:

Director, Club Services
American Advertising Federation
1101 Vermont Avenue NW, Suite 500
Washington, DC 20005
(202) 371-2326
(800) 999-AAF1
Fax: (202) 898-0159

The Retail Advertising and Marketing Association (RAMA) has 1,500 members nationwide. Membership brings you studies of advertising expenditures, a quarterly newsletter, use of the RAMA **Resource Center's** books and videos, discounts on seminars and subscriptions, and a member **directory** that is useful for networking. Contact:

Retail Advertising & Marketing
Association International
500 N. Michigan Avenue, Suite 600
Chicago, IL 60611

The Point of Purchase Advertising Institute (POPAI) includes 850 members who produce and supply point-of-purchase advertising signs and displays as well as national and regional advertisers and retailers who use, and are interested in the effectiveness of, such media. POPAI sponsors award competitions and student programs and maintains a library and **speakers' bureau**. Contact:

Point-of-Purchase Advertising Institute
66 N. Van Brunt Street
Englewood, NJ 07631
(201) 894-8899

The City and Regional Magazine Association's 50 members include not only consumer-oriented publications but related businesses involved in advertising, printing, and circulation. It publishes a quarterly **newsletter** and its monthly *Media Watch* and conducts professional development seminars. Contact:

City and Regional Magazine Association
5820 Wilshire Boulevard, No. 500
Los Angeles, CA 90036
(213) 937-5514

The Business/Professional Advertising Association (B/PAA) lists 40 local groups with a total of 4,500 members. All are business communicators in the fields of advertising, marketing, and marketing communications. The organization sponsors seminars and annual awards. Contact:

Business/Professional
Advertising Association
100 Metroplex Drive
Edison, NJ 08817
(908) 985-4441

Direct Response

The Direct Marketing Association (DMA) membership of 6,800 encompasses the entire range of creators and producers of direct mail and other direct response advertising, from list brokers and compilers to retailers, from envelope manufacturers to ad agencies. Its many services include frequent seminars and **workshops,** a number of publications, annual awards, a library of 2,500 direct-marketing campaigns and 500 reference books, and a government affairs office in Washington. Contact:

Direct Marketing Association
11 West 42 Street
New York, NY 10036-8096
(212) 768-7277

The Advertising Mail Marketing Association (AMMA) works to lobby Congress, the U.S. Postal Service, and the Postal Rate Commission to protect the interests of those who use third-class mail as a medium for advertising and fund-raising. Its membership numbers 450. Contact:

Advertising Mail Marketing Association
1333 F Street NW, Suite 710
Washington, DC 20004-1108
(202) 347-0055

Public Relations

The Public Relations Society of America (PRSA) counts more than 15,000 members. They belong to 100 chapters in 10 geographic districts—the world's largest organization devoted to the practice of public relations. Most chapters schedule regular monthly meetings—luncheons or dinners—with guest speakers or panels. **Workshops** or seminars, guidebooks, audiovisuals, and other materials are offered in the organization's **professional development** program. The research information center at the national office in New York contains a wide variety of informational materials and handles more than 20,000 requests for information and more than 1,000 visitors each year. Contact:

Public Relations Society of America
33 Irving Place
New York, NY 10003-2376
(212) 995-2230
Fax: (212) 995-0757

Women's Organizations

The Women's Direct Response Group (WDRG)—New York Chapter—numbers 600 direct-marketing professionals and works to advance the influence and interests of women in the industry. It sponsors monthly seminars and workshops, a summer **internship** program, and an annual award. Offices are also maintained in Washington and Chicago. Contact:

Women's Direct Response Group
224 Seventh Street
Garden City, NY 11530
(516) 746-6700

Advertising Women of New York (AWNY), founded in 1912, brings together 850 women who hold executive and administrative positions in advertising, publicity, marketing, research, and promotion. It conducts seminars and career clinics and maintains a speakers' bureau. Membership is mostly from the New York City area. Contact:

Advertising Women of New York
153 East 57 Street
New York, NY 10022
(212) 593-1950

Women in Advertising and Marketing

(WAM), with 225 members, meets monthly in Washington. Its professionals network to keep members abreast of developments in marketing and advertising. The club sponsors seminars, a speakers' bureau, and a **job bank.** Contact:

Women in Advertising and Marketing
4200 Wisconsin Avenue NW
Suite 106-238
Washington, DC 20016
(301) 369-7400

What Should I Be Reading?

Books on Advertising and Marketing

Following are brief descriptions of books you may find helpful:

Backer, Bill. *The Care and Feeding of Ideas.* New York: Random House/Times Books, 1993. Adman Backer, of Bates Worldwide, on how anyone can make ideas work in his or her business.

Clancy, Kevin J., and Robert S. Shulman. *The Marketing Revolution.* New York: HarperBusiness (HarperCollins), 1991. Former executives of the Yankelovitch Clancy Shulman research firm on how to think freshly about your current marketing practices.

Gregory, James R., with Jack G. Wiechmann. *Marketing Corporate Image: The Company as Your Number One Product.* Lincolnwood, IL: NTC Business Books, 1991. How decision makers and marketers aggressively promote companies to their many audiences by advertising "corporate image" as their number one product.

Gumpert, David E. *How to Really Create a Successful Marketing Plan.* Boston: Inc. Publishing, 1992. Practical advice from the former editor of the *Harvard Business Review* and now senior editor of *Inc.* magazine.

Hopkins, Claude. *Scientific Advertising.* New York: Chelsea House, 1980. This is the classic basic advertising book, with an up-to-date introduction by John E. O'Toole, former president of the Foote, Cone & Belding agency. Renowned adman David Ogilvy has said, "Nobody, at any level, should be allowed to have anything to do with advertising until he has read this book seven times."

King, Norman. *Big Sales from Small Spaces.* New York: Facts On File, 1986. Tips and techniques for small-space advertising. Essential information on creating and placing small-space ads, based on the fact that 27 percent of U.S. retail sales result from small-space advertising.

Ries, Al, and Jack Trout. *The 22 Immutable Laws of Marketing.* New York: HarperBusiness (HarperCollins), 1993. The latest word from the "positioning" inventors.

Schultz, Don E., and Stanley I. Tannenbaum. *Essentials of Advertising Strategy.* Lincolnwood, IL: NTC Business Books, 1988. This 100-page paperback cuts to the heart of what it takes to produce good advertising based on sound strategy. Its eight chapters cover the process from general marketing plan to final creative execution.

Direct Response

Recent years have produced a number of good books on this specific category of advertising and marketing.

Bencin, Richard L., and David J. Jonovic. *Encyclopedia of Telemarketing.* Englewood Cliffs, NJ: Prentice Hall, 1989.

Bird, Drayton. *Commonsense Direct Marketing.* 2d ed. Lincolnwood, IL: NTC Business Books, 1990.

Ljungren, Roy G. *The Business-to-Business Direct Marketing Handbook.* New York: American Marketing Association, 1989.

Muldoon, Katie. *Catalog Marketing: The Complete Guide to Profitability in the Catalog Business.* New York: American Management Association, 1988.

Roberts, Mary Lou, and Paul D. Berger. *Direct Marketing Management.* Englewood Cliffs, NJ: Prentice Hall, 1989.

Roman, Eman. *Integrated Direct Marketing.* New York: McGraw-Hill, 1988.

Shepard, David. *The New Direct Marketing: How to Implement a Profit-Driven Database Marketing Strategy.* Homewood, IL: Dow Jones-Irwin, 1990.

Newspapers

The two weekly journals of the advertising business are

Advertising Age. Known as "Ad Age," this long-established large-format publication is the flagship of Chicago's Crain Communications, a major publisher of business journals. It is the national newspaper of the business, covering news and offering in-depth features on advertisers, ad agencies, media, and related businesses.

Adweek is oriented chiefly to the agency side of the business but covers news and features on all aspects of the industry. In tone and attitude, it is a sort of cocky kid brother to *Ad Age.*

Direct Marketing is the magazine of the direct response industry, with valuable news and features in that special field, while *Journal of Marketing* and *Target Marketing* cover the entire broad area of marketing.

APPENDIX

For Further Reading

In addition to Schultz and Tannenbaum's *Essentials of Advertising Stategy* and Stone's *Successful Marketing Methods,* which are included in the recommended reading list in Chapter Thirteen, the following books were referred in the presaration of this book.

If you wish to explore the subject of advertising in considerable depth, begin with these four college textbooks:

Dunn, S. Watson, Arnold M. Barban, Dean M. Krugman, and Leonard N. Reid. *Advertising: It's Role in Modern Marketing.* 7th ed. Chicago: The Dryden Press, 1990.

Husted, Stewart W., Dale L. Varble, and James R. Lowry. *Principles of Modern Marketing.* Boston: Allyn and Bacon, 1989.

Nelson, Roy Paul. *The Design of Advertising.* 6th ed. Dubuque, IA: Wm. C. Brown, 1989.

Wells, William, John Burnett, and Sandra

Moriarty. *Advertising Principles and Practices.* Englewood Cliffs, NJ: Prentice Hall, 1989.

Other books referenced were:

Bacon, Mark S. *Do-It-Yourself Direct Marketing: Secrets for Small Business.* New York: John Wiley & Sons, 1992. A guide to low-cost techniques.

Bly, Robert W. *The Copywriter's Handbook.* New York: Henry Holt and Company, 1985. Subheaded "A step-by-step guide to writing copy that sells." Good, practical tips for anyone starting out to write advertising copy.

Cook, Kenneth J. *AMA Complete Guide to Small Business Marketing.* Lincolnwood, IL: NTC Business Books, 1993. A practical book that concentrates on selecting, analyzing, and rating target markets, then developing a sales plan.

Ries, Al, and Jack Trout. *Positioning: The Battle for Your Mind.* New York: McGraw-Hill, 1981. The first book by the best-selling author—and ad men—who first described "positioning" inventors.

Stone, Bob. *Successful Direct Marketing Methods*. 4th ed. Lincolnwood, IL: NTC Business Books, 1988.

Witcher, William K. *How to Solve Your Small Business Advertising Problems.* Aptos, CA: Advertising Planners, Inc., 1986. This 8-inch-by-11-inch workbook is oriented entirely to advertising for retail stores. Organized by media categories, with worksheets in each sections. No index; the "Dictionary of Advertising Terms" at the back lacks a description of the marketing plan. The book does, however, contain an abundance of practical information.

Index

A

N

O

P

Q

R

S

T

U

V

W

X

Y

Z

ABOUT THE AUTHOR

Bernard Ryan Jr., served for seven years as Senior Vice President/Public Affairs of the American Association of Advertising Agencies, the national association of the agency business. Earlier, he was a founder of Wilson, Ryan & Leigh, Inc., and served as that agency's chairman of the board for six years. Before that, he was a Creative Supervisor at Batten, Barton, Durstine & Osborn (BBDO) in New York City for 15 years. Mr. Ryan has written widely in advertising, public relations, early childhood education, biography, and true courtroom dramas. His 12 published books include *So You Want to Go into Advertising,* a career guide for young people. He has also ghostwritten six published books. He and his wife, Jean, live in Southbury, Connecticut. They have two daughters and two grandchildren.

MADE SIMPLE BOOKS

For almost four decades, *Made Simple* books have set the standard for continuing education and home study. In answer to the changing needs of today's marketplace, the *Made Simple* series for the '90s presents a thoroughly up-to-the-minute portfolio of skills, information, and experience, with revised and updated editions of bestselling titles.

Made Simple books are available from your local bookstore. You may also order direct (make a copy of this form to order).

Titles are paperback, unless otherwise indicated.

ISBN	TITLE	PRICE		QTY		TOTAL
23280-2	Accounting	$12.00/$15.00 Can	X	______	=	______
47556-X	Advertising for a Small Business	$12.00/$16.95 Can	X	______	=	______
23938-6	Arithmetic	$12.00/$15.00 Can	X	______	=	______
26582-4	Astronomy (Third Edition)	$12.00/$15.00 Can	X	______	=	______
23882-7	Bookkeeping	$12.00/$15.00 Can	X	______	=	______
19427-7	Business Letters	$12.00/$16.00 Can	X	______	=	______
47557-8	Business Law	$12.00/$16.95 Can	X	______	=	______
18850-1	Chemistry	$12.00/$15.00 Can	X	______	=	______
26586-7	Citizenship	$12.00/$16.00 Can	X	______	=	______
41639-3	Desktop Publishing	$11.00/$14.00 Can	X	______	=	______
17483-7	English	$12.00/$15.00 Can	X	______	=	______
41638-5	Estate Planning	$11.00/$14.00 Can	X	______	=	______
47466-0	Freelancing	$12.00/$15.95 Can	X	______	=	______
26521-2	French	$12.00/$16.00 Can	X	______	=	______
19911-2	German	$12.00/$16.00 Can	X	______	=	______
42429-9	Growing Your Small Business	$12.00/$15.00 Can	X	______	=	______
00437-0	Intermediate Algebra and Analytic Geometry	$12.00/$16.00 Can	X	______	=	______
00736-1	Italian	$12.00/$16.00 Can	X	______	=	______
41339-4	Latin (Revised Edition)	$12.00/$15.00 Can	X	______	=	______
26794-0	Learning English	$12.00/$16.00 Can	X	______	=	______
26584-0	Mathematics	$12.00/$15.00 Can	X	______	=	______
46894-6	Money, Banking, and Credit	$12.00/$16.95 Can	X	______	=	______
41804-3	Office Management	$12.00/$15.00 Can	X	______	=	______
46934-9	Perfect Business Plan, The	$12.00/$15.95 Can	X	______	=	______
42533-3	Philosophy (Second Edition)	$12.00/$14.95 Can	X	______	=	______
24228-X	Physics	$12.00/$15.00 Can	X	______	=	______
41428-5	Secretarial Practice	$9.95/$12.95 Can	X	______	=	______
42552-X	Small Business Franchise	$12.00/$15.00 Can	X	______	=	______
18818-8	Spanish	$12.00/$15.00 Can	X	______	=	______
26642-1	Spelling	$12.00/$16.00Can	X	______	=	______
02355-3	Statistics	$12.00/$15.00 Can	X	______	=	______
19426-9	Touch Typing	$12.95/$15.95 Can	X	______	=	______
41786-1	Wall Street	$12.00/$15.00 Can	X	______	=	______
19618-0	Word Power	$12.00/$16.00 Can	X	______	=	______
23742-1	Your Small Business	$12.00/$15.00 Can	X	______	=	______
	Shipping and handling (add $2.50 per order)		X	______	=	______
		TOTAL				______

Please send me the title(s) I have indicated above. I am enclosing $ __________.
Send check or money order in U.S. funds only (no C.O.D.s or cash, please). Make check payable to Bantam Doubleday Dell. Allow 4 - 6 weeks for delivery. Prices and availability are subject to change without notice.

Name: ____

Address: ____________________________________ Apt. #: __________

City: ______________________ State: ________ ZIP Code: __________

Send completed coupon and payment to:
Bantam Doubleday Dell
ATTN: Distribution Services
Dept. MS01
2451 South Wolf Road
Des Plaines, IL 60018

MADE SIMPLE BOOKS

MS01- 2/96